ROOTED & GROUNDED CHRISTIAN BOOT CAMP

THE RACE TO FINISH WELL HAS BEGUN!

by

Loretta Rich Ministries / GMMW
W/ HOLY SPIRIT Orchestration

B E L I E V E R S
M A N U A L

"GO and Make Disciples of all Nations."
(Matthew. 28:19)

Being Properly Equipped as a Disciple of CHRIST in order to with Confidence Properly Disciple others as I am commanded to do!

Copyright © 2023 by Dr. Loretta Rich Ministries | GMMW

All Scripture quotations are public domain courtesy of Bible Gateway: www.biblegateway.com.

All Rights Reserved. No part of this publication may be reproduced, stored in a retrieval system, or transmitted in any form or by any means, electronic, mechanical, photocopying, or otherwise, without the prior written permission of the copyright owner.

Paperback ISBN: 979-8-9869160-6-4
Library of Congress Control Number: 2023900604

ALL RIGHTS RESERVED
PRINTED IN THE USA

CONTENTS

Dedication	5
About The Author	7
Book Order & Contact	11
Introduction Part A Page	12
Reason Why GOD Should Let You in Heaven & Worksheets	20
Importance of Basic Christian Doctrine	22
Worksheets	27
Go Make Disciples JESUS' Charge to The Church	28

ROOTED & GROUNDED FOUNDATION STONES

Reasons To Know the Six Foundation Stones	29

FIRST THREE DOCTRINAL FOUNDATION STONES

Repentance From Dead Works	30
Faith Towards GOD	32

THE DOCTRINE OF BAPTISMS:

Baptism Into the Family of GOD	33
Baptism In Water / How were You Baptized?	34
Baptism In HOLY GHOST / HOLY SPIRIT	46
Worksheet	83
Introduction Part B	84

LAST THREE DOCTRINAL FOUNDATION STONES

Laying On of Hands	87
The Resurrection of The Dead	91
Prayer To Be Saved & Then What	98
Worksheet	101
Eternal Judgement	103
The Five Crowns	116
Worksheet Assessment & Review	119

DEDICATION

Dedicated to those who desire to finish their spiritual race well by having their spiritual house built on the SOLID ROCK and not sinking sand!

Dedicated to those that have a desire to be a doer of the WORD and not just a hearer only. Those who desire to not only obey the Great Commission by being wise and winning souls for CHRIST, but also desire to know how to properly disciple and teach new believers:

The Doctrine of the Six Foundation Stones is given to the church in accordance with Hebrews 6:1-3. GOD is permitting, giving this opportunity to the church to reassess our understanding of Hebrews 6:1-3. For what purpose? That all can obey Matthew 28:19.

Yes, The Rooted & Grounded Bootcamp Book/Manual is even for those that have been discipled but need a refresher's teaching on the Six Foundation Stones. The Refresher again will be for the purpose of fulfilling the Great Commission, which is **properly making disciples of others**!

Dedicated to those that understand that being JESUS' disciples requires them to make disciples. This Boot Camp Book/Manual is for those who desire to obey the Scriptures found in the Gospel of JESUS CHRIST Matthew 28:19-20, "Go ye and make disciples of all nations," Mark 16:15 "HE Said to them, "Go into all the world and preach the gospel to all creation." In Mark 16:20 (NIV), "Then the disciples went out and preached everywhere, and the Lord worked with them and confirmed His Word by the signs that accompanied it."

Dedicated to **those** who truly want to be: "**The Light of The World**", "**A City on A Hill**" and "**The Salt of The Earth**". Emphasizing, that once **refreshed, refocused**, and **reminded,** of the Rooted and Grounded Six Foundation Stones, **You** Can, with **Greater Confidence, Enthusiasm, Boldness, Joy** and with **Beautiful Feet upon the mountains**, <u>**Go Forth Obeying JESUS, and Making Disciples of Others**</u>**.** Dedicated to those that desire to be steadfast, unmovable, always abounding in the work of the LORD in as much as you know, that your labor will not be in vain in the LORD, (1 Corinthians 15:58). <u>**The LORD sees and rewards!**</u>

ABOUT THE AUTHOR

Apostle, Senior Pastor of Grace & Mercy Ministries, WeightAside, Dr. Loretta Rich's greatest desire and mission, as a Leader in the Body of CHRIST is to show the love of JESUS CHRIST by Teaching, Instructing, and Equipping all Church Leaders, all believers, and those that desire to become believers in CHRIST JESUS the LORD. She feeds, disciples, teaches, and trains JESUS' sheep through the Boot Camp Sessions, Church Fellowships, Bible Study, Bible College, Youth Outreaches, Young Adult Ministry, Radio, Television, "Drama with a Mission," and several other Teaching and evangelistic outreach programs, projects and speaking engagements.

Loretta takes very seriously what the Holy Bible says about all believers being properly discipled, equipped and then, commissioned to **"Go Ye into All the World…!"** The LORD has instructed HIS Church to, "Go into all the world and make Disciples of all nations" (Matthew 28:19). Winning Souls, Preaching the Gospel of Salvation through CHRIST; (Witnessing to the Unsaved), is what the Church is to do but, that is not the end; only the beginning. After souls are saved, they then become a part of the Family of ALMIGHTY GOD. This happens through faith in the Blood of the LORD JESUS CHRIST alone! Now, The New Believers must have a solid foundation upon which to build their New Spiritual House.

Loretta is given a strong mandate by HOLY SPIRIT to help properly disciple the Church of the LORD JESUS CHRIST. This burden was placed on her by the LORD. This perhaps is because HE knows that Loretta understands what it is like to be sincere about church but, to be sincerely wrong. Loretta grew up as a child and young adult attending a very traditional church. She was blessed to know a lot of good hymns and gospel songs. She even did a few solos while in the choir. However, Loretta received no teachings from the Holy Bible regarding her need to repent and accept JESUS CHRIST as SAVIOR and LORD of her life. She thought that trying to be a good person and going to church was all there was to GOD and heaven. She was taught nothing about Salvation and Eternal Life through the accepting of CHRIST JESUS as LORD and SAVIOR.

She thought that being in the choir and attending church would surely guarantee her a place in heaven if she were to pass from this life to the next. Years later, while away from her home church, she was witnessed to. She heard the Gospel for the very first time. She was led in a prayer which involved repentance and asking forgiveness for her sins. She accepted CHRIST JESUS as her personal SAVIOR and LORD.

Loretta began studying the Bible for the first time ever; appalled that up until that day, she was playing church and didn't even know it. Dangerous! Had she died during that time, she would have gone to hell because, as the WORD of GOD declares, "For all have sinned and fall short of the glory of GOD (Romans 3:23). Also, "The wages of sin is death; (total separation from GOD for all of eternity), but the Gift of GOD is Eternal Life through JESUS CHRIST our LORD," (Romans. 6:23). Well, what is the antidote for sin, death, hell, total separation from GOD for all of eternity?

Answer: **The Gift of GOD, THE LORD JESUS CHRIST!** Have you called upon the Name of the LORD JESUS CHRIST to be your personal LORD and Savior?

You can repent and be saved too. Please, make sure that you are not playing Church. Going to the church building does not make us Born Again Christians, even as going to McDonalds or Burger King does not makes us a hamburger. Be sure you are truly saved. Confess with your mouth the LORD JESUS and believe in your heart that GOD raised JESUS from the dead (according to Romans 10:9-10).

Here is a suggested prayer that you can pray, confessing in sincerity out **loud**: "GOD, I repent of my sins. I am turning my life over to YOU Now. I ask YOUR forgiveness for my sins. I am receiving the LORD JESUS CHRIST, YOUR GIFT of Salvation. I accept JESUS, believing that HIS Blood was shed and sacrificed to make payment for my sin debt. JESUS CHRIST, through YOUR death, burial and bodily resurrection, I understand that I am now saved from the penalty of my sin, and I have become a born-again child of GOD. Thank YOU JESUS CHRIST my LORD and SAVIOR. For by Grace, I am now saved through my faith in YOU. I have Eternal Life now, through my Belief on and in YOU, and not on my own good works, merits nor by my church attendance. Hallelujah! LORD, please lead me to the right Church Fellowship that, I may Grow in Grace, get Properly Discipled and become a useful member in the Body of CHRIST. I am a Born-Again Christian because of what YOU accomplished for me. Again, thank YOU JESUS for saving me, and giving me Eternal Life, In JESUS my LORD'S Name I pray. Amen.

Well, if you said that prayer, then today is your Spiritual Birthday! Stick with the Boot Camp Book/Manual for instructions on what to do next. Your Name is written in heaven in what is called "**The Lambs Book of Life**". You are now a New Creation in CHRIST your LORD and SAVIOR. Begin thanking the LORD each day for so, GREAT A SALVATION! Welcome to the BODY Of CHRIST! **Read**: The following Scriptures: ((Romans 10:13, John 3:16-18, Acts 2:38, Ephesians 2:8-9, Romans 10:9-10, Hebrews 2:3, 1 Corinthians 5:17).

How To Order Rooted & Grounded Christian Believer's Bootcamp Book/ Manual

~Discount on Bulk Orders of Three or more

~Order Book(s) On
(202) 880-0507

Amazon, Christian Books.com, Barnes & Nobles, or Order by Phone: (240) 435-9293

~Order through Cash App: $LRGBC5 or $KCMmin22
or
~Write: Loretta Rich Ministries
R&G Boot Camp
P.O. Box 783, Clinton
Maryland 20735
(Please Send Money Order, No Checks)

~Order Additional Copies for Your
~Church Leaders, New Members Orientation, Cell Small Groups, Family Discipleship or Family, Friends, Neighbors, and Personal Boot Camp Session, etc.

For More Information:
Email: loretta.rich@outlook.com or
lorettarich.w8aside@gmail.com
Text or Telephone: (202) 880-0507 or (240) 435-9293
Website: www.weightaside.org

Encouraging, Empowering, and Equipping the Church for Execution...
The Next Move
➡ THE GREAT AWAKENING!

Born Again Believers, we must never forget that "HE which hath begun a Good Work in us, will be Faithful to Complete it in us "Until the Day of Redemption", (The Day of Our LORD JESUS' return to Rapture HIS Church and give us all a Glorified Body) Hallelujah! The FATHER GOD's goal for us, HIS Children, is for us all to mature, endure to the end and be ready at HIS return for us.

Let's remember that nothing can pluck us out of our FATHER GOD's hand and, we do not want to jump out. Nothing can separate us from HIS LOVE. HE is not loving, HE is LOVE. The very essence of LOVE unconditionally, AGAPE. JESUS has provided for us all things that pertain to life and godliness. HE has given us HIS Written WORD; Logos. We have HIS LIVING WORD; Rhema; (the LORD JESUS CHRIST living within Us, BY HOLY SPIRIT). We have more than 72,000 angels at our disposal. We have the GOD kind of faith. We have been redeemed from sin, poverty, sickness and the second death. In CHRIST JESUS we are made Wisdom, Righteousness, Sanctification and Redemption. We are Heirs of GOD and Joint Heirs with the LORD JESUS CHRIST. We are seated with HIM in heavenly places. We have more than 7,000 Promises found in the WORD of GOD. Those Promises are Yea, (Yes) and Amen; (So Be It) for us. We have the Whole Amour of GOD, which enables us to stand against the wiles of the devil. We have the Fruit of the SPIRIT. Yes, in this life, our HEAVENLY FATHER, by CHRIST JESUS our LORD and HOLY GHOST

Orchestration has given us everything, that is necessary for our growth and spiritual maturity. All things that pertain to life and godliness has been given to us in CHRIST JESUS our LORD. Amen? (2 Peter 1:13)

You may personally question the LORD's FAITHFULNESS as, JEHOVAH JIREH our PROVIDER of these things. This may be due to some unforeseen circumstances involving death, relationships, family, finances, employment, dreams deferred; (making your heart sick) and unanswered prayer(s) and so on.

I want to encourage your hearts to press in and not give up, not cave-in and not quit. When the disciples of The LORD JESUS CHRIST were challenged with rather to walk away from JESUS or remain HIS followers, many departed. However, the original 12 disciples took a stand. JESUS asked them if they would depart and turn away from following HIM also.

Peter responded for them all, "Where would we go, for you alone have the WORDS of Eternal Life." (John 6:67-68) How True! They had tasted and seen that the LORD is GOOD! GOD is Good! All the time; and all the _____ GOD is _____!

Let's not be of those that draw back into the world, but rather be like those who will mature and continue to believe until the saving of our souls, (Hebrews 10.39). We must work out our own soul salvation with fear and trembling, (Philippians 2:12-13). We must continue to mature, doing nothing from selfishness, or empty conceit. That we do nothing from factional, (impure) motives or strife. But rather, with an attitude of gratitude and humility; (being neither arrogant nor self-righteous), regard and consider others. We must not just look out for our own interest. We must timidly shrink from whatever would offend GOD, and discredit the LORD JESUS CHRIST, (Philippians 2:4-18). Let us be doers of the WORD and not just hearers only. Remember, we cannot live by bread alone but by every WORD that proceeds from the mouth of GOD. Therefore, as mature believers let's continue to study to show ourselves approved unto GOD, as workmen that need not be ashamed, rightly dividing the WORD OF TRUTH. Let's refrain from fleshly lust of the flesh, lust of the eyes and the pride of life.

In order to finish well, as a HOLY SPIRIT Filled, Equipped Believer; with a Solid Foundation, we <u>must</u> follow those who through faith and patience inherited the promises. They were mature enough to continue pressing towards the mark, for the Prize of the High Calling of GOD, in and through CHRIST JESUS our LORD. (Philippians 3:12-16).

In summary, being an Equipped Christian and Finishing Well, does require each one of us believers to remember that many are the afflictions of the righteous, but the LORD will deliver us out of them all. Being a mature follower of JESUS CHRIST will require us to exercise our Sixth Sense, which is Faith. We must continue to walk by faith and not by sight. The Just <u>Must Live by Faith</u>. This is recorded 4 times in the Scriptures. (Romans 1:17, Galatians 3:11, Hebrews 10:38, Habakkuk 2:4).

We must have a Solid Foundation upon which to build. Finishing Well Believers must remember that the race is not given to the swift, nor to the strong but to those that endure to the end; the same shall be saved. We must run our race and finish our course well. (Ecclesiastes. 9:11).

HINDRANCES TO THE RACE:

Hindrance # 1:

We will not finish well if we are trying to run someone else's spiritual race; converting their gift(s). (Galatians 2:2, Hebrews 12:1, 1 Corinthians 9:24-25)

Hindrance # 2:

We will not finish well if we become weary in well doing. (Galatians 6:9-10, Galatians 5:7)

Hindrance # 3:

We will not finish well if we do not Lay Aside the Weights and the Sins that can so easily beset us, (take us off the course that GOD has for us to, not only run, but finish the race well). (Hebrews 12:1-2, Philippians 2:12-16)

Hindrance # 4:

We will not finish well if we don't run our race with patience, keeping our eyes on JESUS CHRIST, and studying the WORD of GOD. (Hebrews 12:1-2, 2 Timothy 2:15, Matthews 4:4)

Hindrance # 5:

We will not finish well if we do not walk in love and forgiveness. (Ephesians 5:2, 1 John 4:7-8, Colossians 3:13, Matthew 6:14)

Hindrance # 6:

We will not finish well if we: do not walk in the SPIRIT, Live in the SPIRIT, and be Led by the HOLY SPIRIT. (Being filled with HOLY GHOST and yielded to HIM).

Getting in our own lane and, staying the course, to run our own race, is **paramount to our victory of finishing well**. Unlike in a natural race, where only one person can take the First Place Award, every victorious finisher, in the Born-Again Christian race, can receive First Place! However, they must **finish their own spiritual race lawfully, (no cheating) and faithfully (enduring to the end)**.

In our Spiritual Race to Finish Well, we are not in competition with anyone but ourselves. Paul puts it like this: "But I keep under my body, and make it a slave, so that after I have preached to others, I myself will not be disqualified for the prize." (1 Corinthians 9:27)

The New Living Translation puts it this way: "I discipline my body like an athlete, training it to do what it should. Otherwise, I fear that after preaching to others, I might be disqualified." The King James Version (KJV), in this same passage of Scripture, Paul says, after preaching to others, I do not want to become a **"castaway"**.

Do not become weary in well doing. The WORD of the LORD says, "You shall reap if, you faint not." Again, being equipped with a Solid Foundation, upon which to build your spiritual house, is also extremely important, in our race to Finish Well.

As children of GOD, we must be fully persuaded and determined to carry out our GOD given Mission. This would be the Mission which the LORD has ordained for us individually, with each person doing their part. Every joint (person) has something to supply or to contribute by HOLY SPIRIT Orchestration. Each part will make the whole-body function, in the perfection for which FATHER GOD purposed. <u>Every joint must supply their part</u>. Thereby, making up the whole of the Body of CHRIST.

We all have the Ministry of Reconciliation. Yes, we all are called to be witnesses of and for CHRIST JESUS our LORD. Our witness is to be with our lifestyles, words, actions, and the preaching and sharing of the Gospel Message. Once an individual gets saved, we are to disciple them. They would need to become rooted and grounded in the faith. This is done with, "GODfidence" (Confidence in GOD) if, we have been properly discipled ourselves.

Let's remember that the harvest is still plentiful, but the laborers are few. "Go Ye Therefore and make disciples of men…" as JESUS commanded us. This will require that we be properly discipled right ourselves.

In summary, the only thing that can impede or hinder us from not Maturing and Finishing Well is if we haven't been given a Solid Foundation, and or if we forget what we have been given in CHRIST JESUS our LORD. This is an opportunity that the LORD is providing for us. What we are being given is more than enough if we would lay claim on it.

JESUS is returning in the Rapture for a Mature, Victorious, and Glorious Church that have completed their Spiritual Race, Finishing Well!!! Please go through the Rooted & Grounded Bootcamp Manual and Workbook to first, see if you are planted on a Firm Solid Foundation. Then, see if you would benefit more by going through the "Rooted & Grounded Boot Camp (Book) Manual" in our Group Session. Yes, you are also invited to go through this Bootcamp Sessions with me or one of our team members.

Be assured that you are Truly Rooted and Grounded in the Faith making sure that you are equipped, properly discipled and ready to Properly Disciple others.

By the Grace and Mercy of our LORD, we all can continue to mature, having a Victorious Finish to our Spiritual Race. We can be Ready when JESUS Returns for HIS Church. Rewards will be taught in this Rooted & Grounded Bootcamp Manual as well.

Let's Do This! Amen?

On the next page there is a worksheet. Please answer the six questions. The questions are pertaining to being Rooted & Grounded in the Faith, with a Solid Foundation.

This is not to embarrass anyone. You will be taking your own spiritual pulse to see if you are, properly discipled. Can you without a doubt, do what JESUS Said, "**Make Disciples of people" using the Six Foundation Stones found in HIS WORD**?

If not, we are one in the Body of CHRIST, and it is for that reason that JESUS had me do this Rooted & Grounded Bootcamp Manual.

Should CHRIST delay HIS coming, there will be Bootcamp: Workshops, Group Sessions, Leadership Conferences, Church, Bible Study & Cell Group Meetings. Call for more information.

(Scripture References: Philippians 1:6, John 10:28-30, Romans 8:38-39, 1 John 4:16, 2 Peter.1:13, Matthew 26:53, Galatians 3:13, Galatians 3:29, 1 Corinthians 1:30, Romans 8:17, 2 Corinthians 1:20, Ephesians 2:6, Ephesians 6:10-20, Genesis 22:14, John 6:68, Psalm 34:8, 2 Pet. 1:3, Psalm 34:19, Philippians 3:14, Matthew 4:4, Ecclesiastes 9:11, 2 Timothy 2:15, Habakkuk 2:4, Romans 1:17,

Galatians 3:11, Hebrews 10:38, Hebrews. 6:12, 2 Timothy. 4:7, Ephesians. 5:27, Mark 16:15-18)

Encouraging, Empowering, and Equipping the Church for Execution…
The Next Move
 **THE GREAT AWAKENING!**
ROOTED AND GROUNDED IN THE FAITH
PART I
FIRST THREE FOUNDATIONAL STONES
HOLY SPIRIT'S <u>EQUIPPING</u> ALL BELIEVERS… AND YOURSELF!!!

1. If GOD were to ask, "Why should HE let you into HIS Holy Heaven?" What would your answer be?

_____
_____
_____
_____
_____

2. Do you believe that you are a <u>Useful Member</u> in the Body of CHRIST; making <u>Full Proof</u> of your ministry?
Yes _____
No _____

3. Do you think that every Believer is <u>Rooted and Grounded in their Faith</u>?
Yes _____
No _____

4. Do you think that it is dangerous, for a Believer not to be Rooted and Grounded in their Christian Faith & the Six Foundational Doctrines?

Yes _____

No _____

If YES then, what are some of the dangers? Explain and support your answer with two Scriptures. **(Use additional paper if needed)**

_____
_____
_____
_____
_____

If NO, explain and support your answer with two Scriptures. **(Use additional paper if needed)**

_____
_____
_____
_____
_____

5. Do you believe that you are truly Rooted and Grounded in the faith?

Yes _____

No _____

If YES, please explain what it means to be Rooted and Grounded in your faith and the Six Foundational Doctrines?

_____
_____
_____

If NO, do you believe that it is your fault or, the fault of your Spiritual Overseer(s)? Or a combination of both?

_____
_____
_____
_____
_____

Basic Christian Doctrine is very important! It determines how strong or weak your foundation is. When a house is not founded on a firm foundation, then it is prone to fall, when strong winds or a storm beats upon it. The taller the building the deeper the foundation needs to be to support the structure. A house with part of a foundation, or even half of a foundation, is just as dangerous. It too will not stand for long.

As with a natural building or house, so it is with our Spiritual House. In Matthew 7:24-27, Jesus speaks of the House Founded on Sinking Sand verses or contrasted with the House Founded on the SOLID ROCK. HE said the Wise Man or Woman builds their Spiritual House on the SOLID ROCK. Therefore, when the winds, storms and troubles of life beat upon that Spiritual House, it will stand firm amidst it all. Why? Because it is founded upon the SOLID ROCK.

The LORD has given us six very essential Doctrinal Foundation Stones upon which to lay a firm foundation. These six doctrinal stones will provide the believer with the foundation that is needed to build their Spiritual House upon. Doctrine means teaching, instruction, education, and explanation. A Doctrine is a statement about a specific Truth.

Where Doctrinal Truths are Rooted and Grounded in the Christian Believer's Life, then finishing the Spiritual Race, remaining faithful, enduring until the End as an Overcomer, becomes very possible! These Six Foundation Stones will enable the Believer to be firmly planted in the Faith. The believer will have the confidence needed, to even defend the Faith without fear or uncertainty.

On the contrary, without the Six Foundation Stones being properly laid, many Christians will remain babies in CHRIST. They never really become mature, useful members in the Body of CHRIST. Some even depart from the faith being easily offended. Some depart from the faith given heed to seducing spirits and doctrines of devils. Some are weak in the faith and dare to share or witness to the unsaved. Many feel inadequate to even defend their faith when challenged.

We wonder why many Christians, that confess the Sinner's Prayer, even receiving JESUS CHRIST as LORD and SAVIOR, can sometimes remain very carnally minded; (still have a worldly mind set, nonproductive, church goer but, only bearing little to no Spiritual Fruit. Why are they unable or unwilling to make disciples for CHRIST? JESUS has commanded the believers, in the Book of Matthew, Chapter 28:11-20 and Matt. 9:35-38, to reap HIS harvest, right? Could it be that their spiritual foundation was never properly, or completely been laid? Therefore, they do not know how to obey that command.

The Holy Bible speaks of the **four kinds of soils** that the WORD of GOD falls on. In Matthew 13:1-23, Mark 4:1-20, Luke 8:1-15, each lets us know that the WORD, which is the seed, falls on different grounds (soils). The ground is the heart of an individual. One such ground, that the WORD, (which is the Seed) falls on is, **by the wayside**, another **on stony ground**, and **on thorny ground**. However, only one type of heart is **good ground**.

I believe there is hope for the other three, heart / grounds. I believe that if the others would get properly Rooted & Grounded in the faith, with the Six Foundation Stones properly being laid in their lives, they too would be given a better chance for the WORD, (Seed) to take root in their hearts. Yes, the three grounds, I believe could have a better chance of becoming Good Ground. This is if they could really get Rooted and Grounded in the initial, laying of their Spiritual Foundation.

Faith comes by hearing the WORD. Therefore, I sincerely believe, and have witnessed that in accordance with the total teaching of the foundational doctrines that are found in Hebrews 6:1-2, the possibility of the three bad soils can be changed. to good ground.

I believe at least some among the three bad grounds, if not all of them, can become useful members in the Body of CHRIST. Yes, becoming a part of the Glorious Church, awaiting JESUS' appearing in the rapture. All of this is very likely, if they would be willing, to get in the Bootcamp.

There is a very real possibility that the Truth, the Seed of the WORD of GOD, can break up that fallow ground of the wayside, stony, and thorny ground (heart). The term, "**Break up that fallow ground**," is taken from Hosea 10:12 and Jeremiah 4:3. The meaning is, **do not sow your seed among thorns**." Break, sever, detach, disassemble, pull off, all your fleshly, worldly, bad, and evil habits. Clean, clear out, remove, eliminate, get rid of, dispose of, and pull up from the roots the weeds. Weed out, eradicate, and exterminate from your hearts the weeds. This is in order for the heart, which is "the ground, yes, the soil" may be prepared for the seed of GOD's WORD of righteousness to be planted... Getting Rooted & Grounded, with a Solid Foundation from Hebrews 6:1-2, can pull up from the roots the weeds. The WORD can clean up and remove the **wayside, stony, and thorny hearts (grounds)**.

Ephesians 5:26, let us know that we are cleansed by the washing of water, by the WORD (of GOD). I truly believe, that if those three bad soil grounds / hearts where to sit under the foundational Doctrinal Truths, that they too, could become good ground. Being Rooted & Grounded in the Faith, with a Solid Foundation upon which to build and grow, is very possible. If the three bad grounds (hearts) would avail themselves to the WORD of GOD, that builds faith and cleanses from sin then they too, can become good ground. The LORD can take out the stony, thorny and wayside heart, and give them a heart of flesh. (Ezekiel 36:26, Jeremiah 31:33; and Hebrews 8:10)

There is hope for everyone. All must be willing to get Rooted & Grounded in the Foundational Truths that will establish a solid and firm foundation to build upon. (Isaiah 28:16, Ephesians 2:19-22).

Hebrews 6:3, tells us that GOD is permitting the basic foundational truths to be revisited. Why? Because HE knows that many have skipped them, or have never been discipled, instructed, educated, or taught Hebrews 6:1-2.

In some church circles, believers were just exposed to the meat of the WORD; right after being Born Again. Therefore, without a spiritual foundation being laid first, some are falling from the faith. Again, this is due in large part to not having a Spiritual Foundation laid. Once properly laid, all can go on unto perfection; not having to lay the foundation again.

You will never see a builder tearing down a home that has a perfect foundation in order to rebuild another one. However, the properly discipled believer can go back to get a refresher's study of Hebrews 6:1-2, in order to disciple others that need it. Remember, Discipled Believers are to become Disciplers.

There is No Condemnation, but How EQUIPPED ARE YOU? How Strong Is Your Foundation? Have you personally understood, experienced, and learned what being Rooted and Grounded in your Faith, is Truly All About? The Bible, the WORD of GOD seems to believe that a Solid Christian Foundation is SO…IMPORTANT that there are approximately 132 Scripture References on it. Read a few here: Matthew 7:24-27, Luke 6:47-49, 1 Corinthians 3:13-16.

QUESTION & ANSWER WORKSHEET

1. What happens, if like a natural building, a Christian's spiritual house is not founded, or built on a solid foundation? (Refer to Matthew 7:26-27)

_____
_____
_____
_____
_____

2. Summarize Luke 6:47-49

_____
_____
_____
_____
_____

3. What does the word "doctrine" mean?

_____
_____
_____
_____
_____

4. With doctrinal truths, and being Rooted and Grounded in the Christian faith, what becomes possible in the spiritual life of that Believer?

_____
_____
_____

5. Contrary to question #4, as a Born-Again Believer, what are the results of not being educated, taught, and instructed in The Six Foundation Stones, in Hebrews 6:1-2?

_____
_____
_____
_____
_____

6. Be honest, have you been properly discipled? No shame. But do you have the assurance that you can properly disciple others with the doctrines found in Hebrews 6:1-2?

_____
_____
_____
_____
_____

JESUS SAID, "GO MAKE DISCIPLES," MATTHEW 28:19; NOT JUST WIN THE SOULS AND LEAVE THEM.

So then, what are the Six Foundation Stones upon which each Spiritual House is to be built upon? Once this foundation is laid properly, the good news is that it will not have to be laid again. As with a natural house, that has a good foundation, it will not have to be torn down and rebuilt. Please remember however, that there are times when GOD will permit us to go back to review the six foundation stones even after you have been properly discipled. In most cases, it will be to remind you of them. Why? Because we must, "Go Ye" and make disciples for HIM.

The Six Foundation Stones:

So, what are the **Six Foundation Stones** in Hebrews 6:1-2?

"Now leaving the Principles of the Doctrine of CHRIST, let us go on unto Perfection, (maturity) not laying again (Once laid properly, you don't have to lay them again remember?) the foundation of...

1. REPENTANCE FROM DEAD WORKS
2. FAITH TOWARDS GOD
3. DOCTRINE OF BAPTISMS
4. THE LAYING ON OF HANDS
5. THE RESURRECTION OF THE DEAD
6. ETERNAL JUDGEMENT"

Hebrews 6:3, "And this will we do, if GOD permits."

GOD is permitting us to do this because, there is an Urgent Need for a Proper Spiritual Foundation to be laid in every believer's life!

In the chapters, I will define each Foundation Stone. Please, do your part, even if you feel you already know and understand these Six Stones. Study and review them. Let this be the standard by which you disciple others that they may have their Spiritual Foundation laid.

The goal of our FATHER GOD is that we be properly discipled, in accordance with Matthew 28:18-20, and then, **go and make disciples.** Disciples are made and not born. We are made disciples by becoming trained, taught, instructed, and educated in the Foundational Doctrinal Truths of the WORD of GOD. Disciples, are to be taught, educated, and instructed in how to follow and apply the doctrinal truths of Hebrews 6:1-2.

The First Foundational Stone is…
"REPENTANCE FROM DEAD WORKS"

What does it mean to repent from dead works? All must repent of trying to earn their place in heaven. No amount of good deeds, good works, or good behavior can qualify us to have eternal life in heaven with GOD, The HOLY FATHER.

Therefore, going to Church for an example, **Does Not Save Us.** Neither does it make us a Christian. Going to McDonalds does not make us a hamburger, right? Well, going to church does not make us a Christian or a child of GOD.

Getting water baptized, singing in the choir, helping others, being kind, being a good person, praying, having a family member as a preacher, giving to the poor or needy, none, I repeat, none of those deeds will qualify us to earn heaven.

Remember this question? If GOD SHOULD ask you, "Why should I let you into MY Holy Heaven?" What would be your answer? If your answer, is any of the above reasons then, you have answered incorrectly. You would not get to heaven on your own merits or goodness. All the good that we can do on our own to try and earn heaven are called Dead Works. The Bible says that all of the right things that we try to do to get to heaven and be saved amounts to "Filthy Rags" (Isaiah 64:6).

We must know that and teach others. Why? Because we have "All Sinned and come Short of the Glory of GOD", (Romans 3:23). Therefore, we must Repent (turn away from trying to earn Salvation and a right to heaven). We cannot clean ourselves up, no matter how good we believe that we are. The only way to get to GOD and Eternal Life in Heaven is to Believe on the ONE HE sent to die in our place, for our Sins. There is a payment that must be paid for our Sins. For the Wages (payment) of Sin is Death. (Romans 6:23). JESUS CHRIST is the GOD Given GIFT for all. HE died in our place and through Faith in HIM as LORD and Savior we get forgiven and washed in HIS Shed Blood. We are to Repent, (turn away from trying to earn our own way to heaven). Repent means to turn from our Sins and humbly turn ourselves over to JESUS to Wash us in HIS BLOOD, cleansing us and making us New Creatures (New Creation) in HIMSELF. "Therefore, if any man be in CHRIST, he is a new creature. Old things have passed away and behold, all things are become new," (2 Corinthians 5:17).

Ephesians 2:8-9 makes it very clear that "For by Grace (Unmerited Favor), we did not earn or deserve it. We are Saved and that not of ourselves it is a GIFT of GOD, not of Works (our human efforts) lest we should boast (brag and be prideful). Therefore, we Repent of the Dead Works of trying to earn our own way to heaven.

Now, we are to do Foundation Stone number Two…

Move in "**FAITH, TOWARDS GOD**." We simply put our Faith in what GOD has done, on our behalf. The Belief and Trust in the Father GOD that HE has sent us HIS ONLY BEGOTTEN SON, to be the Propitiation (Sacrifice) for our Sins, (1 John 4:10). Having Faith Towards GOD is the belief in what GOD said that HE has done for us, the human race. "GOD SO LOVED THE WORLD THAT HE GAVE HIS ONLY BEGOTTEN SON, THAT WHOSOEVER BELIEVETH IN HIM SHOULD NOT PERISH, BUT HAVE EVERLASTING LIFE." (John 3:16). We must personally have faith in what GOD has done. Again, GOD has given us the LORD JESUS

CHRIST to die and pay the penalty for our sins. We deserved death, hell, and the grave. The wages (the payment we owe) for our sins is death; total separation from GOD for all of eternity. We must have faith to believe that the LORD JESUS CHRIST died in our place, was buried, went to hell, and arose from the dead on the third day, according to the Scriptures. Faith towards GOD is simply to have faith in WHO, HE has given as our sin sacrifice.

JESUS' Life was given in exchange for our death, hell, and the grave. We only have to believe and receive the GIFT of the LORD JESUS CHRIST. Accept the LORD JESUS CHRIST. Romans 10:13 declares, "For whosoever shall call upon the Name of the LORD (JESUS) Shall be saved," (delivered from the wages, penalty of their sin). Also, Romans 10:9-10, Amplified Bible declares: "Because if you acknowledge and confess with your mouth that JESUS is LORD (recognizing HIS Power, Authority and Majesty as GOD), and believe in your heart that GOD raised HIM from the dead, you will be saved," (from your sin debt, forgiven, delivered from death, hell and the grave; which is the payment everyone deserves for our sins). Acts 2:38, "Then Peter said unto them, repent and be baptized every one of you for the remission (forgiveness) of sins, and ye shall receive the gift of the HOLY GHOST," (HOLY SPIRIT ONE and the SAME).

Once you have first repented, then confessed with your mouth JESUS as your personal SAVIOR and LORD, believing in your heart that GOD raised HIM from the dead, you become A Born-Again Christian. Your spirit becomes alive, which means quickened by the SPIRIT of GOD. You are now a New Creation. Your old sinful nature from Adam has now been crucified with CHRIST (Galatians 2:20). It's no longer you that live, but CHRIST JESUS who lives in you.

You have the second Foundation Stone laid properly and are ready for **Foundation Stone Three**...

"THE DOCTRINE OF BAPTISMS," Baptisms is plural, indicating that there is more than one Baptism for the Born-Again Believer. Yes, once saved, you become a child of the MOST HIGH GOD. Yeah!!! You are now, **(A.) BAPTIZED INTO THE FAMILY OF YOUR HEAVELY FATHER; GOD HIMSELF.** You have become baptized into GOD's family with sisters and brothers in CHRIST. In 1 Corinthians 12:13 it states, "For by one SPIRIT are we all baptized into one body, whether we be Jews or Gentiles, whether we be bond or free; and have been all made to drink into one SPIRIT," (Share in, or partake of one SPIRIT.). In John Chapter 3, JESUS addresses a man name Nicodemus, {Please, read all of John Chapter 3}. JESUS tells Nicodemus that he must be Born Again in order to become a part of GOD'S family, GOD's Kingdom. John 3:5 "Very truly I tell you, no one can enter the kingdom of God unless they are born of water and the Spirit. (See repeated below verses 4-8)

"Nicodemus saith unto HIM, How can a man be born when he is old? can he enter the second time into his mother's womb, and be born? Jesus answered, Verily, verily, I say unto thee, Except a man be born of water and of the Spirit, he cannot enter into the kingdom of God. That which is born of the flesh is flesh; and that which is born of the Spirit is spirit. Marvel not that I said unto thee, Ye must be born again. The wind bloweth where it listeth, and thou hearest the sound thereof, but canst not tell whence it cometh, and whither it goeth: so is every one that is born of the SPIRIT."

Now! (Not Before), do we get **(B.) BAPTIZED IN WATER,** to identify with our SAVIOR, CHRIST JESUS' Death, Burial and Resurrection. As a Believer, getting Water Baptized is your public acknowledgement of your personal faith in JESUS CHRIST as LORD and SAVIOR. Water Baptism is the first act of obedience after being saved. Being immersed (Covered) in Water is signifying a watery grave. Then, you rise up out of the water to walk in newness of life, following CHRIST. (Galatians 3:26-29, Romans 6:3).

Again, having repented from the old life of sin and now, following your new LORD and SAVIOR JESUS CHRIST you are to get immersed in Water Baptism. JESUS HIMSELF Yes, HE was baptized in water by John the Baptist. Matthew 3:16, "As soon as the LORD JESUS HIMSELF was baptized, HE came up out of the water. At that moment heaven was opened and he, (John the Baptist) saw the SPIRIT of GOD descending like a dove and alighting on HIM," The LORD JESUS CHRIST.

Baptism for many has gotten out of order. Many have gotten baptized prior to getting Born Again. Remember the First Foundation Stone, **Repentance from Dead Works**? Anything that we do to try and earn our way to heaven, apart from letting JESUS SAVE us. Does Not Count!!! Getting water baptized before getting saved may have gotten you or someone else membership into a local assembly (church) but, it will not make you or them apart of the true Church of the LORD JESUS CHRIST. The True Church is comprised of the Born-Again Souls, the Body of CHRIST and not a structure or building. Getting water baptized prior to salvation may have made you or someone a member of a particular congregational or denominational family but, not the Family of GOD. You have to be born into GOD'S family. How? Through acceptance of the LORD JESUS CHRIST WHO, is the only MEDIATOR between GOD and man.

(1 Timothy 2:5) "For there is ONE GOD, and ONE MEDIATOR (or Go Between, to bridge the gap) between GOD and mankind, the MAN CHRIST JESUS."

Through JESUS alone, anyone can be saved. Once saved by the Precious Shed Blood of the LORD JESUS CHRIST, then you get Water Baptized in HIS Name. Why? To identify with HIS death, burial, and bodily resurrection. This justifies the believer. If you were water baptized prior to being saved, please get Baptized Again! This time when you do it, you will know that you are saved. You will know the reason why you are getting baptized in Water. It will not be a dead work, once you have been saved and the cart will not be before the horse. Join with JESUS your LORD in Water Baptism as a Scriptural Doctrine (Instructions, Teachings, and education).

Colossians 2:12 says, "Having been buried with HIM (JESUS) in baptism, in which you were also raised with HIM through your faith in the working of GOD, who raised HIM from the dead." Also, Romans 6:1-7 "Well then, should we keep on sinning so that God can show us more and more of his wonderful grace? ²Of course not! Since we have died to sin, how can we continue to live in it? ³Or have you forgotten that when we were joined with Christ Jesus in baptism, we joined him in his death? ⁴For we died and were buried with Christ by baptism. And just as Christ was raised from the dead by the glorious power of the Father, now we also may live new lives. (Walk in newness of life). ⁵Since we have been united with him in his death, we will also be raised to life as he was. ⁶We know that our old sinful selves were crucified with Christ so that sin might lose its power in our lives. We are no longer slaves to sin. ⁷For when we died with Christ, we were set free from the power of sin. ⁸And since we died with Christ, we know we will also live with Him."

It is important to say, that Water Baptism does not save you. If someone dies or just cannot go and get baptized in water due to an illness, etc., that will not keep them out of heaven. Why? Because like the thief on the cross, (during JESUS' crucifixion) he couldn't come down to get baptized. Some are not physically able to get baptized due to sickness or perhaps, just prior to giving their life to CHRIST JESUS the LORD they passed away. In summary, JESUS knows if there is a legitimate reason for not obeying the command and doctrine which is, to get baptized in water. Again, now saved, the believer is to be obedient to the scripture and their first act of obedience is to get baptized in water to identify with CHRIST. This is to be done in the name of JESUS, as soon as possible unless there is a sickness or life and death situation that prohibits it.

WATER BAPTISM IS DONE IN JESUS NAME OR FATHER, SON, AND HOLY GHOST???

Also, as you read through the Book of Acts, the Early Church Baptized everyone in Water in the Name of the LORD JESUS CHRIST. Why? Because HE'S the GIFT of the FATHER GOD to the whole world. HE is the One WHO died in our place.

Yes, JESUS HE died, was buried, and rose again on the third day, for us to become Born Again Christians. It is JESUS that we identify with by Water Baptism.

Scripture References:
Apostle Peter, on the day of Pentecost, was preaching repent to the crowds. "Repent and be baptized in the name of Jesus Christ for the remission (or forgiveness) of sins" (Acts 2:38). This was the only way Water Baptism was done.

Additional Scripture References: Acts 19:5 "When they heard this, they were baptized in the name of the Lord Jesus."

Acts 8:16 "For as yet HE (HOLY SPIRIT) was fallen upon none of them: only they were baptized in the name of the Lord Jesus."

You may be wondering; if the early Apostles, those of whom were the First Church of the LORD JESUS CHRIST, (HIS Body in the earth), did they fully immerse in water, and did they Water Baptize in HIS Name? How did the Apostles and Church Leaders of the early church baptize the new converts, the saved, born-again believers? Yes, the Apostles, fully immersed all of the believers in water and this was all done, in the name of the LORD JESUS CHRIST ONLY. Then, you may ask, why do some denominations baptize in the name of the FATHER, SON, and HOLY GHOST? Very Good Question! This is done primarily because some denominations read in the Book of Matthew 28:19, what they believe JESUS said, and what they interpreted it to mean: "And Jesus came and spake unto them, saying, all power is given unto Me in heaven and in earth. "Go ye therefore, and teach all nations, baptizing them in the name of the Father, and of the Son, and of the Holy Ghost: Teaching them to observe all things whatsoever I have commanded you: and, lo, I am with you always, even unto the end of the world. Amen." (Matthew 28:19)

Does the Scriptures Contradict themselves? Do we baptized in water in the name of FATHER, SON, and HOLY GHOST (HOLY SPIRIT), or do we follow the only way, that water baptism was done over and over again by the early church Apostles; those that walked with JESUS? Be at peace; you have not sinned by asking that question.

I had the same question when I got born again. I heard and had read several explanations from several denominations and people.

I recognized that there were contradictions in their explanations. One thing I did know, was that there are no contradictions in JESUS; WHO is the WORD of GOD made flesh. (John 1:1-14).

Also, JESUS did make the statement in Matthew chapter 28:19.

So, I needed to check in with JESUS. I needed Orders from HEADQUARTER. It was the LORD JESUS CHRIST WHO said,

"And the HOLY GHOST shall be your TEACHER," (John 14:26, Nehemiah 9:20, Luke 12:12, 1 John 2:27, I Corinthians 2:10, 1 Corinthians 2:12-13, Isaiah 11:2).

Therefore, I sought the answer from HOLY SPIRIT. HE, HOLY GHOST, or you can call HIM HOLY SPIRIT (SAME), will lead us into ALL TRUTH, and not some TRUTH.

First thing we must know is that, out of the mouth of two or three witnesses every WORD of GOD is established, (2 Corinthians 13:1, Matt. 18:16, 1 Timothy 5:19).

How many times have the scripture in Matthew Chapter 28:19, been confirmed, by other biblical scriptures? How many times have you read in the scriptures that believers were baptized in the Name of the FATHER, SON, and HOLY SPIRIT?

If you are honest then, your answer would be nowhere else in scripture. Would you agree that Baptism in Water is a Biblical Doctrine (Teaching, Instruction, and Education)? If you said yes, then you are very correct, Excellent! It is a Very Important Church Doctrine to educate, teach, and instruct believers in following. Then, why would it only be mentioned once in scripture that it is done, in the name of the FATHER, SON AND HOLY GHOST? Could it be that the interpretation of that scripture was misunderstood by many denominations and or ministers? Let's compare, not contrast Matthew 28:18-20 in its Context with Acts 2:38-41, which is one of many scriptures of the actual baptizing in water in JESUS NAME.

Matthew 28:18-20, "And Jesus came and spake unto them, saying, all power is given unto Me in heaven and in earth. Go ye therefore, and **teach** all nations, **baptizing them in the name of the Father, and of the Son, and of the Holy Ghost**: **Teaching** them to observe all things whatsoever I have commanded you: and, lo, I am with you always, even unto the end of the world Amen."

Acts 2:38-41, "Then Peter said unto them, Repent, and be **baptized every one of you in the name of Jesus Christ** for the remission of sins, and ye shall receive the gift of the Holy Ghost. For the promise is unto you, and to your children, and to all that are afar off, even as many as the Lord our God shall call. And with many other words did he testify and exhort, saying, Save yourselves from this untoward generation. Then they that gladly received his word were baptized: and the same day there were added unto them about three thousand souls."

I would like to make this clear, I sincerely do not believe that anyone would be kept out of heaven, because they were baptized in the name of the FATHER, SON and HOLY GHOST as opposed to, in the name of The LORD JESUS CHRIST. This is because water baptism did not cause them to become born again in the first place. The believer's repentance, confession of JESUS CHRIST with their mouth, coupled with believing in their heart that GOD raised JESUS CHRIST the LORD from the dead, accomplished that.

Now back to comparing the two scriptures and not contrasting them. There are no contradictions with the scriptures. As with the Doctrine of Baptisms, with an "s" on baptism<u>s</u>, making it plural, in the Book of Hebrews 6:2a, the Messianic Jewish Tree of Life Version of the Bible says, "of **teaching** about immersions…" This is replacing the word baptism with immersions. Again, there are no contradictions in the WORD of GOD, as is seen when we consider the following truths:

JESUS left instructions for us to "Go ye therefore and **TEACH** all nations."

What are we told to **TEACH**? The Baptism<u>s</u>. Confirmed in Hebrews 6:2a: "The Doctrine (teaching, instructions, and education) of "Baptisms."

Please notice again, that Baptism<u>s</u> is plural with an "<u>s</u>". We are instructed to **TEACH** all nations, baptizing in the name of the **FATHER, SON and HOLY GHOST**, which are THREE in the GOD HEAD, Ah! Plural right? The DIETY or GOD HEAD have distinct or different roles that they carry out, in the salvation of the human race. Back to the Scripture, we are told to "**Teach** the nations to observe all things", (See Scripture below, highlighting Matthew 28:18, and verse 20).

"[18]And Jesus came and spake unto them, saying, all power is given unto Me in heaven and in earth. [19]Go ye therefore, and **teach** all nations, **baptizing** them in the name of the Father, and of the Son, and of the Holy Ghost: [20]**Teaching** them to observe all things whatsoever I have commanded you: and, lo, I am with you always, even unto the end of the world. Amen."

Defining Baptism: it means, to be immersed. Immerse, (Definition from Oxford Languages Dictionary) means - "as to involve oneself deeply in a particular activity or interest." Example: "She immersed herself in her work." Immerse also means "to dip or submerge in a liquid." An example would be Water Baptism.

JESUS said, "Go **Teach.**" Further, HE said "**Teach them**, (Who? The nations) to observe all things. What things (Plural)? The Baptism**s**. Very Good, you are correct.

The Doctrine of Baptism**s** is to be **taught**, (Heb. 6:2a). Why the "s" on Baptism**s**? The answer is found in verse 19 of Matthew, Chapter 28. "Baptizing them in the name of the **FATHER, SON** and **HOLY. GHOST.** There are **THREE** in the GOD HEAD: GOD the FATHER, GOD the SON and GOD the HOLY GHOST.

We are to teach the FATHER's part or role in Baptism, the SON's part or role in Baptism, and the part, or role which HOLY GHOST have in Baptism. All THREE, of the GOD HEAD is ONE but, THEIR part or roles are different, as seen in the New Birth of Believers. THEIR roles are to be taught.

Where some in denominations went wrong, (no shame or condemnation) is that:

a. instead of **Teaching the FATHER, SON, and HOLY GHOST's roles in baptism** and…

b. instead of "**Teaching the nations to observe all things**" (Plural); (the **Three** parts of Baptism, in many cases the Church's leaders **taught nothing**.

c. they just started putting people in the water to get baptized. Again, no shame. Prior to HOLY GHOST giving me the answer, I didn't have a clue either. All I knew is that there cannot be contradictions with my HEVENLY FATHER'S WORD with, some denominations baptizing in JESUS Name, and some in the name of the FATHER, SON, and HOLY GHOST.

Therefore, I did not want to be confused. JESUS said in John 14:26, that HOLY GHOST or HOLY SPIRIT (The SAME), would be my teacher. So, I asked HIM. I'm not trying to turn this into a Testimonial however, the truth is, I and my family were baptized in water when I was 9 years old. This was a requirement if my family was to become a member of that particular church. We didn't know anything. We were not taught anything about salvation. (But I thank GOD for the Hymns I learned. Hallelujah! But the hymns couldn't save me huh? Once saved though, I understood the hymns better.)
I did learn a decade later, that my family and I were dry sinners that had gotten baptized in the Name of the FATHER, SON, and HOLY GHOST and, came up out of the water as wet, (very cold - due to the temperature of the water) sinners. According to scriptures, getting baptized would be a dead work if, the person was not Born Again/Saved first. Many have not even been Born Again prior to their water baptism.

We can learn from our mistakes, right? Again, many denominations, etc. went wrong because they did not obey the Scripture in Matthew 28:18-20. Perhaps they never **Taught the Doctrine of Baptisms correctly.**

The GOD HEAD: GOD THE FATHER, GOD THE SON and GOD THE HOLY GHOST, were all involved in the converting of souls from darkness into light and from the power of Satan unto GOD! Yes, The GOD HEAD was all involved in the salvation of sinners. How this happened was to be **taught**.

Remember Foundation Stone Two? "**FAITH TOWARDS GOD**." What was to be taught about Baptizing in the name of the FATHER? What part in the Baptisms did the FATHER have? Well, a person had to have faith and belief towards what the FATHER GOD said that HE did in order to redeem mankind. GOD gave HIS ONLY BEGOTTEN SON as a GIFT to the world, (review Stone # 2).

The FATHER GOD receives and baptized the new believers into HIS Family. This is after they have repented of sin and self-righteousness and accepted HIS GIFT OF ETERNAL LIFE, through JESUS CHRIST HIS SON. Remember the definition of "baptize" is to immerse. One of the definitions of immerse is: "as to involve oneself deeply in a particular activity or interest." Example: "She immersed herself in her work." Well, GOD HIMSELF, immersed HIMSELF into HIS Plan of Salvation. Now, regenerated, saved children are welcomed into HIS Loving Family. New believers are baptized into the Family of GOD; WHO is now their HEAVENLY FATHER. Hallelujah x7!

Without being **baptized in the name of the FATHER (GOD)**; which is being (Immersed) Baptized into HIS Family, the other Baptisms cannot happen. Therefore, there is but ONE Baptism which, leads to the others. Baptized in the name of the SON; JESUS and HOLY GHOST, could not happen without that first Baptism into the FATHER'S Family.

This is why Ephesians 4:5-6 speaks of "One Baptism." It's the one that must be! Without it, there is No Way to have or truly experience the other Two Baptisms. "There is one body, and one Spirit, even as ye are called in one hope of your calling; One Lord, one faith, **one baptism**, One God and Father of all, who is above all, and through all, and in you all." Remember, with FATHER GOD, first things must stay First!"

Again, being Baptized in Water in the Name of the SON and being Baptized in HOLY GHOST follows getting baptized into the FATHER'S family. We are to follow the Scriptures. No one in the early church was baptized in water in the name of the FATHER, SON, and HOLY GHOST. All believers in the early church were baptized in water in the name of JESUS. This was to identify with JESUS' death, burial, and bodily resurrection. Again, the instructions in Matt. 28:18-20 were to **Teach** this Doctrine.

The FATHER, SON, and HOLY GHOST (HOLY SPIRIT) have different roles in the new believer's changed life experience. All THREE experiences are necessary. It is a part of having a Solid Spiritual Foundation.

> "For there are three that bear record in heaven, the Father, the Word (is JESUS, John 1:1-14), and the Holy Ghost: and these Three are One."
> 1 John 5:7

BAPTISM WITH HOLY SPIRIT - RIVER OF LIVING WATER

> The Baptism with the POWER of HOLY GHOST is a part of the Third Foundation Stone: **The Doctrine of Baptisms**. HOLY SPIRIT or HOLY GHOST (WHO is the same PERSON) is also the ETERNAL, THIRD PERSON OF THE GOD HEAD. HE is CO-EQUAL with the FATHER GOD and GOD the SON (JESUS). The HOLY SPIRIT'S role, involvement, or HIS part in the Born-Again Believer's New Birth: SPIRIT Filled Life and Ministry is to be **taught** and **experienced** by all Born Again, Saved Believers. John 7:37-39 (KJV), says, "In the last day, that great day of the feast, Jesus stood and cried, saying, if any man thirst, let him come unto Me, and drink. He that believeth on Me, as the scripture hath said, out of his belly shall flow rivers of living water. (But this spake He of the **Spirit**, which they that **believe** on Him **should receive** for the **Holy Ghost** was not yet given; because that Jesus was not yet glorified.)"

REJECTING HOLY SPIRIT

Some say that Baptism with the HOLY SPIRIT, with the evidence of speaking with other tongues, went out with the Apostles and so did signs and wonders, miracles, and gifts. That same group says, HE (HOLY SPIRIT) is no longer necessary in the church. Let's see, in some of the following Scriptures, JESUS' responses to that rejection of HIS HOLY SPIRIT…

"Ye stiff-necked and uncircumcised in heart and ears, ye do always resist the Holy Ghost: as your fathers did, so do ye."
Acts 7:51 (KJV)

"But they rebelled, and vexed His Holy Spirit: therefore, He was turned to be their enemy, and He fought against them."
Isaiah 63:10 (KJV)

"And grieve not the Holy Spirit of God, whereby ye are sealed unto the day of redemption."
Ephesians 4:30 (KJV)

"Truly *and* solemnly, I say to you, all sins will be forgiven the sons of men, and whatever abusive *and* blasphemous things they utter;" "But whoever speaks abusively against *or* maliciously misrepresents the Holy Spirit can never get forgiveness but is guilty of *and* is in the grasp of an everlasting trespass."
Mark 3:28-29 (Amplified Classic Edition)

"But he that shall blaspheme against the Holy Ghost hath never forgiveness but is in danger of eternal damnation."
(Mark 3:29 in KJV)

Again, JESUS said that those that believe in HIM are not to reject but should receive **HOLY GHOST.** Let's re-examine the Scripture.

Verse 37b, "If any man thirst, let him come unto ME, and drink." Verse 38, "HE that believeth on ME, as the Scripture hath said, out of his belly shall flow **Rivers of Living Water**." Verse 39a, "(But this spake HE of the **SPIRIT**, which they that **believe on HIM should receive:**"

ARE YOU THIRSTY?

JESUS compares the infilling or Baptism with HOLY SPIRIT as a satisfying drink to quench an inner deep thirst or longing. HOLY SPIRIT is the Power of GOD sent to indwell the believer's born-again spirit. Out of their **belly shall flow Rivers of Living Water!**

> "These all continued with one accord in prayer and supplication, with the women, and Mary the mother of Jesus, and with his brethren. [15]And in those days, Peter stood up in the midst of the disciples, and said, (**the number of names together were about a hundred and twenty**)."
> Acts 1:14-15

> "And when the day of Pentecost was fully come, they were all with one accord in one place. And suddenly there came a sound from heaven as of a rushing mighty wind, and it filled all the house where they were sitting. [3]And there appeared unto them cloven tongues like as of fire, and it sat upon each of them. [4]And they were all filled with the Holy Ghost, and began to speak with other tongues, as the Spirit gave them utterance."
> Acts 2:1-4

HOLY SPIRIT brings fulfillment. HE quenches the thirst for identity, purpose and meaning in the life of believers. Without HOLY SPIRIT in our lives, there is no real satisfaction. Without HIM, there is only a longing for more of, who knows what? Nothing really satisfies long term. Therefore, the end result is always a feeling of disappointment and emptiness. Been there. What about you? We are all examples of that kind of existence. Later, we will examine this through the eyes of the Samaritan Women; also known as the woman at the well.

HOLY SPIRIT empowers the believers with the enablement and the ability to carry out what they were created to be and do in this life. HE satisfies our deepest longings. JESUS made it clear that every one of HIS followers, **should receive HOLY SPIRIT and not reject HIM, right?**

HOLY SPIRIT WITHIN THE EARLY CHURCH

The first followers of the LORD JESUS CHRIST didn't have any doubt or questions about whether or not a believer was to be baptized with HOLY GHOST. It was just the opposite. They wanted to know if you have received the HOLY GHOST, since you say you are a believer? They expected all believers to be SPIRIT FILLED with the evidence of speaking in other tongues, as the SPIRIT gives utterance. An example is found in Acts Chapter 19:1-7(KJV):

> "And it came to pass, that, while Apollos was at Corinth, Paul having passed through the upper coasts came to Ephesus: and finding certain **disciples**, ² He said unto them, **have ye received the Holy Ghost since ye believed?** And they said unto him, **we have not so much as heard whether there be any Holy Ghost.** ³And he (Paul) said unto them, unto what then were ye **baptized**? And they said, Unto **John's baptism**. ⁴Then said Paul, John verily baptized with the baptism of repentance, saying unto the people, that they should believe on Him which should come after him, that is, on Christ Jesus. ⁵When they heard this; they were **baptized in the name of the Lord Jesus.** ⁶And when **Paul had laid**

> **his hands upon them, the Holy Ghost came on them; and they spake with tongues and prophesied**. ⁷And all the men were about twelve."

Paul asked a very important question to the disciples in Ephesus. Paul knew that HIS LORD and SAVIOR JESUS CHRIST had said that all that believed should receive the HOLY SPIRIT. So why hadn't the disciples in Ephesus received this gift?

They had not even heard about HOLY SPIRIT.

Paul knew that there had to have been a very good reason for those disciples not knowing about HOLY GHOST. All of the believers had been baptized in HOLY SPIRIT. So, why not they? Paul asked the right question again. Unto what were you (water) baptized? That was it! Come to find out, those disciples were still waiting for the coming of the ONE that John the Baptist spoke of the SAVIOR JESUS CHRIST. Once the disciples of John the Baptist understood that the MESSIAH JESUS had come, as John had said HE would, this put them on one accord with what was expected of them.

Re-read Acts 19:4-7. Now, upon understanding and being enlightened, in summary those disciples were baptized in water in the Name of the LORD JESUS CHRIST. Baptized in HIS name because, HE is the ONE that gave HIS life that, they could be saved and have Eternal Life.

Now, they are on one accord with the other believers. They are Born of the SPIRIT and can now be **BAPTIZED with the HOLY SPIRIT.** Paul laid hands on them, and they received **HOLY GHOST with the evidence of Speaking in tongues and they also prophesied.**

What about you? Have you received the HOLY GHOST since you believed?

Yes _____

No   _____

Why or why not?
_____
_____
_____

JESUS in both Luke 24:49 and Acts 1:8, said that HIS followers were to **wait for the promise of the SPIRIT.** Primarily, this was because they were not to witness to others about HIM, nor start any part of their ministry, until they were filled with HOLY GHOST.

"And behold, I send the **promise** of My Father upon you: but **tarry** (wait) ye in the city of Jerusalem, until ye be **endued** (indwelt) with **power from on high**."
Luke 24:49 (KJV)

"And, being assembled together with them, (JESUS) commanded them that they should **not depart** from Jerusalem, but wait for the promise of the Father,"
Acts 1:4 (KJV)

"For John (the Baptist), truly baptized with water; but ye shall be **baptized with the Holy Ghost** not many days hence."
Acts 1:5 (KJV)

"But ye shall receive **power**, after that the **Holy Ghost is come upon you**: and ye shall be **witnesses unto me** both in Jerusalem,

and in all Judaea, and in Samaria, and unto the uttermost part of the earth."
Acts 1:8 (KJV)

Review Questions

1. Following JESUS' ascension back to heaven, GOD had promised that HE would fulfill HIS Promise.
What was the Promise?

_____
_____
_____

2. How many of JESUS disciples were waiting for the Promise?
_____

3. Why did JESUS tell them to wait?

_____
_____
_____

4. How long did they wait? _____

5. What happened to let you know that the wait was over? Explain using Scripture:

_____
_____
_____

INNER THIRSTING EXPERIENCED BY THE SAMARITAN WOMAN

Remember the woman at the well? She had that deep, inner thirst, which she could not get quenched. She thought that she just needed a man, and that would satisfy her. But the inner longings grew worse. I believe she was thinking, "Surely, this restless, unquenched thirst will end, if I just get with the right person. In her case, the right man.

The WORD of GOD lets us know that this woman went from man #1, to man #2, to man #3, to man #4, to man #5, because her soul was **thirsty**. Despite marrying and divorcing all these men, her inner thirst and deep longing for satisfaction was not satisfied nor quenched with human flesh. So, it appears that she just made up in her mind that the next man would not be a marriage but simply cohabitation. (Sidebar: living with a person, no matter how long, does not constitute or equal a marriage.) JESUS said that the man that she was now living with was not her husband. They were shacking (living in adultery). By now, she was expecting to be disappointed, dissatisfied, and let down again. She may have thought, "I'll just play it safe with number six." Her expectations were in the wrong place, but she did not know that yet.

JESUS met this woman at the well at a very desperate time in her life. She was there during the hotter part of the day. No doubt, she was ashamed and didn't want to be seen in the cool of the day when others would be there drawing water from that well. No doubt, she knew that she was the talk of the town, (Read John 4:3-30, 39-43). However, during that long dialog with the Samaritan woman, JESUS zoomed in to the root of her issues.

Certainly, Jesus could not be a prospect because the woman recognized Him to be a Jew. The Jews had no dealing with ethnically mixed people. However, she was right that she needed someone, but not for her flesh. She needed one that could satisfy her inner thirst; give her life real purpose, meaning and belonging. No human could give her what she was thirsty for. Nor can anyone satisfy our deepest longings and thirst. No one but the same ONE that offered her the "LIVING WATER".

"Then saith the woman of Samaria unto Him, how is it that thou, being a Jew, askest drink of me, which am a woman of Samaria? for the Jews have no dealings with the Samaritans."
Jesus answered and said unto her, if thou knewest the **gift of God,** and who it is that saith to thee, give me to drink; thou wouldest have asked of Him, and He would have given thee **living water."**
John 4:9-10

"JESUS said to her, "But whosoever **drinketh** of the **water** that I shall give him **shall never thirst;** but the **water** that I shall give him shall be in him **a well of water springing up into everlasting life"**. "The woman saith unto Him, Sir, give me this **water,** that I **thirst not,** neither come hither to draw."
John 4:14-15

Now, in verse 16, it appears that JESUS was taking a side bar or getting off of the subject when he asked her to, **"Go call your husband."** She had asked JESUS in the above 15th verse, to give her this **Water** that she thirst not, neither come to draw water again."

By the way, JESUS was very much on point by asking her to get her husband. Like with everyone that comes to JESUS for the LIVING WATER, which quenches the inner thirst they have, they must first come to the end of themselves. Repent, acknowledge you are a sinner, and accept CHRIST as LORD and SAVIOR. Why? Because HOLY SPIRIT cannot dwell in an unclean temple. There are no short cuts. The Samaritan Women had to come the right way. Some other way would make her a thief and a robber, according to John 10:1. GOD is no respecter of person.

The woman at the well admitted that she had no husband. JESUS was pleased with her answer. Why? Because it was the truth. JESUS can only deal with the truth. Remember, HE IS THE WAY, THE TRUTH, AND THE LIFE, (John 14:6). In HIM there is NO darkness at all. Liars can't tarry in HIS presence unless they are repenting, (Psalm 101:7).

In verse 18, JESUS told the woman that she had, had five husbands; and the man she now has, is not her husband.

She had been living in adultery with all of them accept, perhaps the first husband. For sure she was now shacking with the last man. This attempt to quench her thirst wasn't working.

However, JESUS didn't condemn her. She was born in sin, even as every human being. This was due to the fall of Adam in the garden, (Genesis Chapter 3). But thank GOD, for the Second Adam; JESUS WHO paid our sin debt, Hallelujah!

On the contrary, JESUS did bring this woman to the place, where she could see her wrong and could confess her need for change. **There is only help for those that admit that they need it. That they had been wrong and that they needed a SAVIOR. That is having a change of heart and mind, repenting.**

The inner thirst cannot be satisfied or quenched with money, worldly status, people, beauty, etc. We all can think of people, perhaps even ourselves, who have acquired or possessed all or some of life's finest things. Yet, they remained thirsty and dissatisfied, with some people even living very short destructive lives. Those things did not satisfy or quench their deep inner thirst.

JESUS is offering **Only ONE WAY, ONE THIRST QUENCHER,** to the woman at the well. She had gone from man to man because her soul was thirsty for: identity, affirmation, acceptance, approval, belonging, worth, and a satisfying purpose for which to live.

What are some of the things you did or do, in an attempt to quench your deep inner thirst? It could be a good thing like working on a job, but you became a workaholic, feeling beat down with no real life.

List some of your attempts to quench your inner thirst apart from CHRIST?

_____   _____
_____   _____
_____   _____
_____   _____

Some, like the Samaritan Woman, think they can only be fulfilled if they marry. However, if you have not settled your thirst issue prior to marriage, then a spouse cannot quench it for you, nor you for your spouse. Marriage takes three. Your life must be sold out to CHRIST and your spouse's life sold out to CHRIST. If you are not happy and content prior to marriage, then you will not be after marriage. Marriage is not for cowards. It's hard work for the two to become one but, it is even more of a challenge without CHRIST being the

Center of both spouses' lives. This has to be not just in words (wedding vows), but indeed as well.

JESUS put this encounter with the Samaritan Woman in the Scriptures for our learning and admonition. Each one of her marriages, according to even today's statistics, proves that the duration gets shorter and shorter each time the person remarries. When someone walks away from their Covenant Vows, it becomes easier and easier for them to, walk away from any other marriage partner. They marry someone else, only to quit, give up and cave in. Each time, staying committed shorter and shorter periods of time. Why?

The unrealistic expectation that a human can fill the GOD-Shaped Void in our hearts, is one of the biggest lies that the devil has told. LOVE Is GOD, and GOD is LOVE. Without HIS definition of LOVE, which is to be shed abroad in the heart of the believers by HOLY GHOST (Romans 5:5), then there is only the lust of the flesh, the lust of the eyes, and the pride of life. Scripture says that the flesh profits nothing; it is the SPIRIT that quickens (makes alive). The divorce court would be empty if marriages were centered in the GOD Kind of LOVE that Never Fails.

As with the woman at the well, everyone must come to realize that the <u>LIVING WATER</u> that is spoken of here is HOLY SPIRIT. JESUS said that we "<u>Should receive HIM</u>."

> Again, it was very necessary for JESUS to emphasize, John 7:37-39, "In the last day, that great day of the feast, Jesus stood and cried, saying, **if any man thirst**, let him come unto me, and **drink**. **He that believeth in me, as the scripture hath said, out of his belly shall flow rivers of living water**. (But this spake he of the **Spirit, which they that believe on him should receive**…"

Great News! The woman at the well, YES, the Samaritan Woman's life was forever changed! In John 4:25-26 JESUS reveals to the woman that HE is the long-awaited MESSIAH who had told her the truth. She accepted JESUS and received, flowing out of her belly the LIVING WATER, the SPIRIT. She drank from the SPIRIT LIVING WATER, and her thirst was finally quenched. The kind of true HOLY SPIRIT LOVE, that satisfies the inner thirst and brings identity, affirmation, acceptance, approval, purpose, meaning and significance yes, she was fulfilled. No more shame or hiding from the public. A genuine new Creation, she did become. Let's look at what she did immediately after being changed…

> "The woman then left her waterpot, and went her way into the city, and saith to the men, Come, see a Man, which told me all things that ever I did: is not this the Christ? Then they went out of the city and came unto Him."
> John 4:28-30 (KJV)

> "And many of the Samaritans of that city believed on Him for the saying of the woman, which testified, He told me all that ever I did. So, when the Samaritans were come unto Him, they besought Him that He would tarry with them: and He abode there two days. And many more believed because of His own word; and said unto the woman, now we believe, not because of thy saying: for we have heard Him ourselves, and know that this is indeed the Christ,

the Savior of the world. Now after two days He departed thence and went into Galilee." John 4:39-43 (KJV)

Now, because of the Samaritan Women's SPIRIT led life, which gave her new directions, she went out into the city as a bold witness of CHRIST. Talking about making disciples!

She testified of JESUS to those in her city. Many Samaritans knew that this woman, must be telling the truth because they saw a Big Change in her life. She would have never really saw them face to face, nor would they have seen her, due to her shame. Shame kept her in hiding. But NOW! The Samaritans in the city came running to meet JESUS based on her testimony. Afterward they to drink. They believed on JESUS, and received the thirst quencher, the RIVER OF LIVING WATER, HOLY SPIRIT!

The ONLY ONE, WHO is offering LIVING WATER to everyone, is crying out "If any man (human) thirst, let him come unto ME, and drink. He that believeth in ME, as the Scripture hath said, out of his belly shall <u>flow RIVERS</u> of <u>LIVING WATERS</u>. John 7:39, lets us know that HOLY SPIRIT is WHO JESUS is referring to. HOLY SPIRIT was to come after CHRIST'S death, burial, resurrection, and ascension back to heaven, glorified.

Maybe you're wondering, "Why does nothing really quench the thirst within me?" You've tried and kept trying different things, natural things and people, etc. It only left you ashamed, disappointed, empty, and still longing for, you don't know what.

However, the Samaritan Woman said she wanted the drink of LIVING WATER that JESUS offered her. She was thinking in the natural of course. Looking for natural water to quench her inner thirst. JESUS spoke of the RIVER OF LIVING WATER, HOLY SPIRIT, WHO did come to live in her.

She is completely satisfied and fulfilled. Are you?
Yes _____
No _____

Think and ponder…

I. JESUS and every Born-Again Believer is given **Birth** by HOLY SPIRIT. Mary Conceived JESUS by HOLY SPIRIT. HOLY SPIRIT quickens (make alive) the Born-Again Believer's Spirit that had died due to Adam's fall.

A. The HOLY SPIRIT'S Work in The Earthly Birth Of JESUS

HOLY SPIRIT is credited with giving Birth to the MESSIAH, JESUS CHRIST. JESUS was conceived in the Virgin Mary. As JESUS came to earth, HE took on an earthly, fleshly body. By coming into the earth as a man, JESUS identified with the human race that HE could become their sin sacrifice, (Philippians 2:6-8).

The Virgin Mary was the vessel that GOD had chosen to bring JESUS, the MESSIAH into the world. Mary did not doubt what GOD had said through HIS messenger, the angel Gabriel. Mary did believe that she would conceive and bring forth GOD'S SON. Her only dilemma was, how? Mary wanted to know how she could have a baby. She was a virgin. How was it to happen seeing that she knew not a man intimately? The angel Gabriel told Mary that she would conceive and give birth to the JESUS the SON of GOD by HOLY SPIRIT.

> "Then, said Mary unto the angel, how shall this be, seeing I know not a man? ³⁵And the angel answered and said unto her, **The Holy Ghost** shall come upon thee, and the power of the Highest shall overshadow thee: therefore, also that holy thing which shall be born of thee shall be called the Son of God."
> Luke 1:34-35 (Read all of Luke Chapter One)

B. The HOLY SPIRIT'S Work in The **Birth of The Born-Again Believer into The Family Of GOD**

In like manner HOLY SPIRIT also gives Birth to the Born-Again Believer in CHRIST JESUS their RISEN LORD and SAVIOR. JESUS told Nicodemus in John 3:7, "Marvel not that I said unto you, **"You must be Born Again."** All Born Again Believers are birthed by HOLY SPIRIT into the Family of GOD, through faith in The LORD JESUS CHRIST.

> "Jesus answered, Verily, verily, I say unto thee, except a man be born of water and of the **Spirit**, he cannot enter into the kingdom of God. ⁶ That which is born of the flesh is flesh; and that which is **born of the Spirit is spirit."**
> John 3:5-6

II. JESUS and every one of the early church believers **waited** until they had been **Baptized** with **HOLY GHOST POWER** before starting their earthly ministries.

A. JESUS' **Baptism with HOLY GHOST** prior to beginning HIS ministry. JESUS, at the age of 30 years old, had to **wait** until HE was Baptized with HOLY GHOST POWER before starting HIS earthly ministry. Yes, it is recorded in Scripture; all Four Gospels declares that the **SPIRIT descended and abode upon JESUS CHRIST**, after HE had been Baptized in Water by John the Baptist.

The Baptism of JESUS as recorded in Mark 1:9-11:

> "In those days Jesus came from Nazareth of Galilee and was Baptized by John in the Jordan. And when He came up out of the water, immediately He saw the heavens being torn open and the Spirit descending on Him like a dove. And a voice came from heaven, "You are my Beloved Son; with You I am well pleased."

Now, in John's Gospel, John the Baptist was told by GOD that he would confirm, that it would be JESUS CHRIST if the SPIRIT like a dove would descend upon HIM. John speaking in…

> I myself did not know Him, but the reason I came baptizing with water was that He might be revealed to Israel. Then John testified, "I saw the Spirit descending from heaven like a dove and resting on Him. I myself did not know Him, but the One Who sent me to baptize with water told me, 'The Man on Whom you see the Spirit descend and rest is He who will baptize with the Holy Spirit. I have seen and testified that this is the Son of God."
> John 1:31-34 (BSB)

The quiet, low key way of living was over for JESUS. JESUS' life would never be the same again. The name JESUS was a very common name among the Jewish people. JESUS is **"YESHUA"** in the Greek. But from that day forward until HIS exit from planet earth, HE will not only be JESUS, but JESUS CHRIST The LORD. (CHRIST means the **ANOINTED ONE and HIS ANOINTINGS**). According to pursuegod.org, LORD in the Hebrew language is **YAHWEH** (meaning that GOD is Eternal and self-existent. HE has always been GOD and always will be). Remember JESUS CHRIST the LORD is, "The WORD Made Flesh, and The WORD Is GOD, i.e., GOD the SON. (John 1:1, 14, 18)

Also…

> "Philip said to Him, "Lord, show us the Father and then we will be satisfied." Jesus said to him, "Have I been with you for so long a time, and you do not know Me yet, Philip, nor recognize clearly who I am? Anyone who has seen Me has seen the Father. How can you say, 'Show us the Father?' Do you not believe that I am in the Father, and the Father is in Me? The words I say to you I do not say on My own initiative or authority, but the Father, abiding continually in Me, does His works [His attesting miracles and acts of power]."
> **John 14:8-10AMP**

Hallelujah X7!

The Mission for coming to this earth "**Was On!**" Again at 30 years old having received HOLY SPIRIT, JESUS was now operating by the POWER and Authority OF HOLY SPIRIT! JESUS CHRIST The LORD, or you can say, The LORD JESUS CHRIST was Ready!!!

Again, following The LORD JESUS CHRIST's Baptism with HOLY GHOST, it was really time for HIM to be about HIS FATHER's Business. HIS Ministry had begun. Sacrificing 40 days with fasting while getting tempted by the devil, as is recorded in Luke 4:1-14, was only the beginning of what HE would endure for all of mankind. JESUS had received HOLY GHOST POWER, and this was certainly needed in order for HIM to do the Ministry that FATHER GOD had called HIM to. Powered by the SPIRIT enabled HIM and will every believer, to stand against the wiles, temptations of the devil!

HE was well fortified now for the Mission, which was prophesied in Isaiah Chapter 61, and in Luke 4:18-21. The LORD JESUS CHRIST declared: Luke 4:18-21 (KJV)…

> "The Spirit of the Lord is upon Me because He hath anointed Me to preach the gospel to the poor; He hath sent Me to heal the brokenhearted, to preach deliverance to the captives, and recovering of sight to the blind, to set at liberty them that are bruised, to preach the acceptable year of the Lord. And He closed the book, and He gave it again to the minister, and sat down. And the eyes of all them that were in the synagogue were fastened on Him. And He began to say unto them, this day is this scripture fulfilled in your ears."

B. The Church, the believers had to <u>wait</u> until they were **Baptized with HOLY GHOST POWER**, before starting their ministry.

In like manner, JESUS instructed the 120 of HIS Believers to **wait** in Jerusalem until they were endued with Power from on HIGH.

They had to <u>wait</u> until they were Baptized and Filled with HOLY GHOST prior to starting their witnessing ministry for and of HIM.

First Outpouring of HOLY SPIRIT:

JESUS had been with HIS 120 disciples for 40 days, following HIS resurrection. On the 40th day, just prior to HIS ascension to heaven, JESUS gave them instructions to go and wait for the PROMISE of HOLY SPIRIT. Out of obedience to their LORD, they went to Jerusalem and waited. On the tenth day of them waiting, HOLY SPIRIT came and filled each of them to include the women. They all had the evidence. They all began to speak with other tongues, as the SPIRIT gave them utterance. This is what happened as recorded in Acts 1:1-12, 14 and Acts 2:1-4.

> ¹The former treatise have I made, O Theophilus, of all that Jesus began both to do and teach, ²Until the day in which he was taken up, after that he through the Holy Ghost had given commandments unto the apostles whom he had chosen: ³To whom also he shewed himself alive after his passion by many infallible proofs, being seen of them forty days, and speaking of the things pertaining to the kingdom of God: ⁴And, being assembled together with them, commanded them that they should not depart from Jerusalem, but **<u>wait</u>** for the promise of the Father, which, saith He, ye have heard of Me. ⁵For John truly baptized with water; **<u>but ye shall be baptized with the Holy Ghost not many days hence.</u>** ⁶When they therefore were come together, they asked of Him, saying, Lord, wilt thou at this time restore again the kingdom to Israel? ⁷And He said unto them, it is not for you to know the times or the seasons, which the Father hath put in His own power. ⁸**<u>But ye shall receive power, after that the Holy Ghost is come upon you: and ye shall be</u>**

witnesses unto me both in Jerusalem, and in all Judaea, and in Samaria, and unto the uttermost part of the earth. ⁹And when He had spoken these things, while they beheld, He was taken up; and a cloud received Him out of their sight. ¹⁰And while they looked steadfastly toward heaven as He went up, behold, two men stood by them in white apparel; ¹¹Which also said, Ye men of Galilee, why stand ye gazing up into heaven? this same Jesus, which is taken up from you into heaven, shall so come in like manner as ye have seen him go into heaven. ¹²Then returned they unto Jerusalem from the mount called Olivet, which is from Jerusalem a sabbath day's journey. ¹³These all continued with one accord in prayer and supplication, with the women, and Mary the mother of Jesus, and with His brethren.

In conclusion, JESUS was birthed by the SPIRIT and before starting HIS earthy ministry at 30 years old, HE was baptized and filled with HOLY SPIRIT's Power to carry out the work of the FATHER.

BENEFITS FROM RECEIVING HOLY SPIRIT BAPTISM

HOLY SPIRIT Empowers the believers to become **Witnesses** of and for the LORD JESUS CHRIST their SAVIOR. HOLY GHOST enables the believers to be an example of CHRIST not just in word and deed, but also in their lifestyle.

HOLY SPIRIT was spoken of in the Old Testament and the New Testament by the prophets of GOD. One such prophecy, given from GOD in the Old Testament by the Prophet Joel, is recorded in the Book of Joel; Joel 2:28, **"And it shall come to pass afterward, *that* I will pour out MY SPIRIT upon all flesh and your sons and daughters shall prophesy…"** This was Prophecy regarding HOLY

SPIRIT's coming to baptize and indwell Born Again Believers in CHRIST JESUS their LORD. This prophecy was also prophesied of by JESUS' Forerunner, John the Baptist. Matthew 3:11**,** "I indeed baptize you with water unto repentance: but HE that cometh after me is mightier than I, whose shoes I am not worthy to bear: **HE shall baptize you with the Holy Ghost, and with fire:**

HOLY SPIRIT was the Promise that GOD said would come. The Promise was that following JESUS' death, burial, bodily resurrection, and ascension back to heaven, HE would send HOLY SPIRIT to be poured out upon the believers. The prophecy was fulfilled; it did happen. HOLY GHOST came exactly the way that FATHER GOD had said. GOD said that HIS.HOLY SPIRIT would come to fill the believers, HE will live in them and seal them unto the day of redemption, (CHRIST'S return for them in the Rapture).

"And **do not grieve the Holy Spirit of God**, with whom you were sealed for the day of redemption." (Ephesians 4:30)

In light of the truth that HOLY SPIRIT lives within the believer, the **Warning** goes out from FATHER GOD, "**DO Not Grieve The HOLY SPIRIT Of GOD…**" Meaning do not irritate, vex, or enrage HIM. HOLY SPIRIT Is completely gentle. HE lives in the believer. However, HE will not push HIS way, therefore the believer must yield to HIM. When the believer engages in any unwholesome activity it grieves HOLY SPIRIT. Remember, HE lives in the believer and has to witness everything that is said and done. HOLY SPIRIT gets irritated when taken into environments where Satan, instead of GOD is getting glory out of the believer's life. Alcohol, drugs, cigarettes, acts of sexual immorality, lies, etc. has vexed HOLY SPIRIT because HE knows, that the Scripture says, "And such were some of you," **past tense.** HE knows the sacrifice that CHRIST endured to give the believer a new sinless nature as a new creation in CHRIST. HE knows that if the believer would just get the mind renewed on the WORD and take advantage of HIS POWER and Grace: (GOD's Enablement, GOD's Empowerment and GOD's Ability, then the believer would represent the FATHER and JESUS Well! HE wants to help but the believer must ask for HIS help! (1 Corinthians 6:11, 2 Corinthians 5:17), HOLY SPIRIT is **PARACLETE or PARAKLETOS,** Greek Word for HOLY SPIRIT as the believer's: **Advocate, Comforter, Counsellor, Helper, Intercessor, Standby, and Strengthener**, (John 14:16).

PARACLETE also denotes that HOLY SPIRIT works parallel, side by side with the believer. Basically, HE says, **I am at your service if you need or ask me to get involved**. HE does not push the believer, but on the contrary, HE leads and guides the believer into, not some but into all Truth. This is when HE is invited to do so. HOLY GHOST is nothing like Satan, who pushing, harasses, tempt, and try to force people to do his evil bidding.

You know, without JESUS finishing his part in the salvation of the human race, the Promise of HOLY SPIRIT coming to live in and empower believers could not had happened. **<u>JESUS is therefore so worthy to receive all glory, honor and praise because of HIS obedience to GOD, even down to HIS death on the Cross.</u>**

"⁵Let this mind be in you, which was also in Christ Jesus: ⁶Who, being in the form of God, thought it not robbery to be equal with God: ⁷But made himself of no reputation, and took upon him the form of a servant, and was made in the likeness of men: ⁸And being found in fashion as a man, he humbled himself, and became

obedient unto death, even the death of the cross. ⁹Wherefore God also hath highly exalted him and given him a name which is above every name: ¹⁰That at the name of Jesus every knee should bow, of things in heaven, and things in earth, and things under the earth; ¹¹And that every tongue should confess that Jesus Christ is Lord, to the glory of God the Father."
Philippians 2:5-11

JESUS' finished work on the Cross was HIS role in accomplishing salvation. HE was slain and raised to life to redeem the believers to GOD; out of every people, tribe, language, and nation, (Revelation 5:9). Whosoever will, can come to HIM by faith. (John 3:16, Ephesians 2:8-9.

This order in which the FATHER GOD does things is highly essential. The Doctrine of Baptisms should truly remind everyone of that TRUTH. FATHER GOD had to do HIS part in the salvation of mankind. CHRIST JESUS THE LORD had to accomplish HIS part. Then, HOLY SPIRIT could and is still accomplishing HIS role or part in the believer's completed work of their salvation until the day of redemption.

> Everything must happen in GOD's ordained order. The WORD of GOD even tells us to do all things decently and in order.
> 1 Corinthians 14:40
> **"Let all things be done decently and in order".**

According to Bible Gateway, this scripture means that: **"We should do things in the proper sequence and at the right time, rather than in a haphazard and impulsive manner."**

Well, the prophecies from GOD were fulfilled because CHRIST JESUS did finish HIS work of providing salvation. JESUS offers this "**So Great a Salvation**" to all. And HE tells us not to neglect it...

"How shall we escape, if we neglect **So Great Salvation,** which at the first began to be spoken by the LORD, and was confirmed by them that heard HIM; GOD also bearing them witness, both with signs and wonders, and with divers miracles, and gifts of the HOLY GHOST, according to HIS OWN will?"
Hebrews 2:3 (KJV)

HOLY SPIRIT IS MORE THAN SPEAKING IN OTHER TONGUES

Some believe that HOLY SPIRIT only enables the believer to speak in other tongues. That is incorrect. The evidence of being SPIRIT BAPTIZED or SPIRIT Filled is you begin to speak with other tongues as the SPIRIT gives you what to utter. I didn't under this as a new believer many years ago.

I thought HOLY SPIRIT would throw open my mouth and do the speaking through me. I know you knew better but I did not. The LORD told me to go back and re-read Acts 2:4…

HE said, "**And they were filled with the HOLY GHOST, and began to speak with other tongues**, as the SPIRIT gave them utterance."

Once Baptized with HOLY GHOST, the now SPIRIT FILLED believer becomes the TEMPLE of the HOLY GHOST. Therefore, great reverence is to be given to the way you the believer carry yourself. GOD's very OWN SPIRIT is living within the believer. HE's the same SPIRIT that raised JESUS from the dead that is now living in the Body of CHRIST, the Church. Yes, HOLY SPIRIT is more than Speaking in Tongues but that is the entry way to all of the benefits below:

+ By HOLY SPIRIT, the believer receives a new Spirit, and new heart, (Ezekiel 36:26-27).

+ Receive the SPIRIT of ADOPTION whereby we cry ABBA FATHER, (Romans 8:15).

+ Believer Sealed with HOLY SPIRIT's Guarantee that CHRIST will be returning for the believer; HE is engaged to Marry HIS Bride. (Ephesians 1:13).

+ Believers receives POWER after HOLY GHOST has come upon them to be a Witness of CHRIST JESUS, (Acts 1:8).

+ HOLY SPIRIT is The Comforter, Teacher, HE brings all things to the believer's remembrance whatever JESUS said, (John 14:26).

+ HOLY SPIRIT also helps our weaknesses by praying and making intercessions (praying) for us, when we do not know what to pray, (Romans 8:26).

+ Gives Songs of Deliverance, (Psalm 32:7).

+ Enables Worship In Spirit & Truth and in the Beauty of Holiness, (John 4:23-24, Psalm 96:9).

+ HOLY SPIRIT sheds the LOVE of GOD abroad in our hearts, (Romans 5:5).

+ Believers have the Fruit of the SPIRIT (see Gal.5:22-23) because Believer is the Temple of HOLY GHOST, (1 Corinthians 6:19).

+ HOLY SPIRIT gives the Ministerial Gifts as HE wills and Spiritual Gifts, (Ephesians 4:11, 1 Corinthians 12:28).

All of this and so much more is given to SPIRIT FILLED, HOLY GHOST Baptized Believer. This Great Salvation is being offered to every human being to either receive it, or reject it. Remember the second Foundation Stone, "<u>**FAITH TOWARDS GOD**</u>"? If you are not Born Again, please take the time to receive CHRIST JESUS as your **personal** LORD and SAVIOR now. <u>**Dying without making JESUS the LORD of your life means death and hell (Total separation from GOD forever)**</u>.

You are just a **prayer** away from having real purpose and meaning to your life. One step away from the promise of Eternal, Everlasting Life, John 3:16-17.

WHAT TO PRAY: (Out Loud): LORD JESUS CHRIST, I believe that YOU are the SON of GOD. I believe that GOD sent YOU into the world to die on the Cross. I understand that this was in order to save me from the penalty of my sins. I believe that you paid for the punishment that I deserve for the sins I have committed. Yes, YOU suffered for ALL of the wrong things I have done. YOU paid with YOUR own BLOOD, so that I could be released from my sin debt. YOU gave up YOUR LIFE in order to give me Eternal Life in Heaven. I believe what the WORD of GOD says in Romans 3:23,

"All have sinned and come short of the glory of GOD," (Come short of GOD's glorious standards). Also, I believe Romans 6:23 that tells me that "The wages (or payment) of sin is death, (total separation from a HOLY GOD). I know this is what I deserve for my sins; (death, total separation from GOD forever). This same Scripture tells me that GOD, however, gave YOU, LORD JESUS CHRIST as a GIFT of Eternal Life instead of that death. Also, Romans 10:13, lets me know that I can call upon YOU, LORD JESUS CHRIST and be Saved. I am calling upon you Now! I ask YOUR forgiveness as I repent, (turn away) from my sins. I believe in my heart and accept YOU as my LORD WHO died, was buried but rose again on the third day, according to the Scriptures. Thank YOU, LORD JESUS, for saving me. I am now <u>Born Again</u>. Hallelujah! (Acts 2:38, Romans 10:9-10). It's time to get Baptized in Water.

<u>Congratulations</u>! Because you have accepted JESUS CHRIST as Your LORD and SAVIOR, the angels in heaven are rejoicing. Now, your name is written in the Book of Life in Heaven.

<u>Review</u>: **Keep in mind that**, just before JESUS' ascension back to heaven, just before HE exited planet earth, HE told HIS followers to go to Jerusalem and **<u>wait</u>** for the promise of the FATHER; WHO is HOLY SPIRIT.

> "And, (JESUS) being assembled together with them, commanded them that they Should not depart from Jerusalem, But wait for the promise of the Father, which, saith He, ye have heard of me. For John truly baptized with water: but you shall be baptized with the HOLY GHOST not many days from now."
> Acts 1:4-5

HOLY SPIRIT is the Comforter, in JESUS absence from earth. Therefore, JESUS said in John 16:7, "Nevertheless I tell you the truth; It is expedient for you that I go away: for if I go not away, the Comforter will not come unto you; but if I depart, I will send HIM unto you."

Also, John 14:26, "But the Comforter, which is the Holy Ghost, whom the Father will send in my name, He shall teach you all things, and bring all things to your remembrance, whatsoever I have said unto you." Also, John 14:16, And I will pray the Father, and He shall give you another Comforter, that He may abide with you forever…"

JESUS, following HIS resurrection from death, told HIS disciples that they would receive Power after that the HOLY GHOST is come upon them, and they would be HIS witnesses in all the world. Acts 1:8-9, "But ye shall receive Power, after that the Holy Ghost is come upon you: and ye shall be witnesses unto ME both in Jerusalem, and in all Judaea, and in Samaria, and unto the uttermost part of the earth. And when He had spoken these things, while they beheld, He was taken up; and a cloud received Him out of their sight."

No doubt, JESUS' followers being 120 in number, to include the women were so excited, (Acts 1:12-15). They, having now spent 40 days with JESUS following HIS resurrection from death. No, JESUS did not do a drive-by, quick one visit to earth, following HIS resurrection. Yes, HE spent 40 days in which HE was still preparing HIS disciples for the moment when HE would be taken out of their presence. (Acts 1:2-3).

HIS followers still needed to **wait** before going to share the Gospel, Good News about the Resurrection and Salvation in CHRIST JESUS their LORD. They heard HIM, saw HIM do many miracles, signs, and wonders, and be resurrected on the third day. As HE told them. However, they still needed to receive HOLY SPIRIT's indwelling power and fire to become witnesses of, and for JESUS. Yes, the 120 Believers had, by the SPIRIT been birthed into the family of GOD the Father. They had experienced the new birth but, now after 10 days of their waiting, on one accord (no confusion, etc.), they were baptized in HOLY SPIRIT. This happened on the Day of Pentecost. (Please Read the entire account in the Book of Acts Chapter 2).

THE EVIDENCE THAT THE 120 WERE FILLED WITH HOLY SPIRIT

How did the 120 believers know that they were Baptized in HOLY GHOST or HOLY SPIRIT? Yes, Correct, Perfect; **they all spoke in tongues as the SPIRIT gave them utterance.**

"And they were all (the 120) filled with the Holy Spirit and began to **speak in other tongues as the Spirit gave them utterance.**
Acts 2:4 (ESV)

"All of them were filled with the Holy Spirit and **began to speak in other tongues as the Spirit enabled them**."
Acts 4:12 (NIV)

MY PERSONAL QUESTIONS, STRUGGLES, AND DILEMMAS REGARDING BAPTISM WITH HOLY SPIRIT

I alluded to this earlier, but perhaps my personal testimony can provide answers for those that may also have questions, and or some confusion with what to believe regarding the Baptism with HOLY GHOST, etc.

After I received JESUS CHRIST as my Personal LORD and SAVIOR, I was told by two different ministries different things. One Ministry said HOLY SPIRIT with the evidence of speaking in other tongues was for the Apostles of old and not for the church today. That Ministry also said that people that claim to have HOLY SPIRIT climbed up on chairs and tore things up in the church, while saying that they had the HOLY SPIRIT moving in them. As a newborn baby in the LORD yes, a now Born-Again believer, hearing this report sounded really strange and somewhat even scary because I was a very reserve type of person. The other ministry taught that if you didn't have HOLY SPIRIT's Baptism with the evidence of speaking in other tongues, then you were none of HIS (GOD'S). As a new convert I wasn't sure what to believe. Therefore, I took my questions to GOD in JESUS NAME. I went home, sat down on my sofa with my BIBLE and asked my LORD; WHO saved me to teach me.

My #1 Question: Do I need HOLY SPIRIT; and does HE cause people to speak?

#1 Answer: The LORD led me through the Old Testament and through the New Testament. HE showed me from Scriptures several examples of HOLY SPIRIT moving upon different individuals in the BIBLE and in every instance from both Testaments, the people spoke. Some prophesied, some spoke with other tongues.

Conclusion: So, it was Biblical and JESUS' New Testament Church were all Baptized with HOLY GHOST. The only way they knew that they were Spirit Filled was because they all spoke with other tongues; that was the evidence.

My #2 Question: Why is the evidence of being HOLY SPIRIT Filled speaking in tongues? Why can't we just clap our hands, raise our arms or something else to show we have HOLY GHOST? Why speak in another tongue, I further asked?

#2 Answer: The LORD led me to the Book of James in the Holy Bible Chapter 3:2-12, "For in many things we offend all. If any man offends not in word, the same is a perfect man, and able also to bridle the whole body.

³Behold, we put bits in the horses' **mouths**, that they may obey us; and we turn about their whole body. ⁴Behold also the ships, which though they be so great, and are driven of fierce winds, yet are they turned about with a very small helm, whithersoever the governor listeth. ⁵Even so the **tongue** is a little member, and boasteth great things. Behold, how great a matter a little fire kindleth! 6And the **tongue** is a fire, a world of iniquity so is the **tongue** among our members, that it defileth the whole body, and setteth on fire the course of nature; and it is set on fire of hell. ⁷For every kind of beasts, and of birds, and of serpents, and of things in the sea, is tamed, and hath been tamed of mankind: ⁸But the **tongue** can no man tame; it is an unruly evil, full of deadly poison. ⁹Therewith bless we God, even the Father; and therewith curse we men, which are made after the similitude of God. ¹⁰Out of the same **mouth** proceedeth blessing and cursing. My brethren, these things ought not so to be. ¹¹Doth a fountain send forth at the same place sweet water and bitter? ¹²Can the fig tree, my brethren, bear olive berries? either a vine, figs? So can no fountain both yield salt water and fresh.

Conclusion: The LORD revealed to me that every person's tongue is untamed, unruly, evil, boastful, blessing one minute and cursing the next, etc. Although mankind has tamed ships and horses that are way bigger than they are yet, mankind cannot tame his own tongue. Verse One again states: "For in many things we offend all. **If any man offend not in word, the same is a perfect man, and able also to bridle the whole body.**" The LORD revealed to me, Why the Speaking in unknown Tongues? HOLY SPIRIT tames the tongue of the believer for the first time, when the believer is SPIRIT Filled. When that happens, the believer is no longer in control of the words coming forth out of the mouth. The Evidence that HOLY SPIRIT has Baptized and Filled the temple / body of the believer, (Sealed it until the day of redemption or JESUS CHRIST'S RETURN For HIS Church), is that the believer speaks a language that was not learned and that is not the native language of the believer. The soul which consists of the mind, will, intellect, emotions, and the imagination, **is NOT in control** of the tongue. The soul cannot discern what's being said. HOLY SPIRIT gets a hold of that unruly tongue that offends, and HE gently bridles it. Now, that it's bridled, the **whole body,** (which JESUS CHRIST the LORD is the HEAD of) can now be brought into subject to obey the HOLY SPIRIT'S leading. Believers are told to Walk in the SPIRIT, Live in the Spirit and be Led by the SPIRIT. If the tongue remained unbridled, then the whole body would be unbridled and not subject to CHRIST by HOLY GHOST Orchestration.

Isaiah Chapter 6:5-9, is an Old Testament example of the tongue getting tamed / bridled, prior to GOD using the vessel namely, Isaiah the Prophet. Remember what the Prophet Isaiah said about himself and the people around him? "Woe is me! for **I am undone**; because **I am a man of unclean lips**, and I dwell in the midst of a **people of unclean lips: for** …"

Remember how the Prophet Isaiah could not be used by GOD to preach to the people, until his tongue got bridled. Isaiah said, "[6]Then flew one of the seraphim unto me, having a live coal in his hand, which he had taken with the tongs from off the altar:[7] And he **laid it upon my mouth**, and said, Lo, this hath **touched thy lips**; **and thine iniquity is taken away, and thy sin purged**." This tongue taming brought Isaiah's whole body under subjection to GOD. Which made him subject to GOD and usable by GOD. Isaiah said, [8]"Also I heard the voice of the Lord, saying, whom shall I send, and who will go for us? Then said I, **here am I; send me**. [9]And He (GOD) said, Go, and tell **this people, hear ye indeed, but understand not; and see ye indeed, but perceive not.**

Puzzled #3 Question: Wow, I was grateful that the LORD answered all of my questions. I understood the reason for speaking in other tongues as evidence. I sincerely desired to be Baptized with HOLY SPIRIT now. I would sit still after praying to receive HOLY SPIRIT, but nothing happened. At my job I begin to take my lunch breaks and go up to the top floor of the building. It was quiet and there would be no one coming up there unless they were going to the roof. I sat on the steps and prayed to receive HOLY SPIRIT, but nothing happened all week. I did not know why.

Question #3: I asked the LORD, "Why didn't I receive the Baptism with HOLY GHOST, with speaking in other tongues?" At home I asked the LORD again. This time HE told me to go back and re-read Acts 2. The fourth verse jumps out at me. "[4]**And they were all filled with the Holy Ghost, and began to speak with other tongues, as the Spirit gave them utterance.** I saw my problem! "**They began to speak** with other tongues, as the **Spirit gave them utterance.**" I had been thinking that HOLY SPIRIT was going to swing open my mouth and begin to speak through me. I see now! Thank YOU, LORD! They spoke but HOLY SPIRIT gave them what to utter. I was to use my vocal cords and give voice to what HE, HOLY GHOST enabled me to say. I opened my mouth, and HE filled it. HE needed me to speak out what I heard being uttered.

Truly at that point out of my belly did flow Rivers of Living Water, HOLY SPIRIT.

PRAYER TO RECEIVE HOLY SPIRIT / HOLY GHOST

FATHER, YOU said in John 7:37-39, that if I thirst, I can come to YOU and drink. FATHER, I am thirsty, and I come to YOU now, to drink. I believe on YOU, as the Scripture has said. Therefore, I expect that out of my belly, shall flow RIVERS of LIVING WATER. I know that this, YOU spoke of the SPIRIT, which you further said, I should receive. I do receive HOLY SPIRIT, WHO is given for me.

FATHER also in Luke 11:13, YOU said, that, "If I, (apart from YOU) then, being evil, know how to give good gifts unto my children: how much more, shall YOU, my HEAVENLY FATHER give the HOLY SPIRIT to me that ask YOU? I ask YOU now FATHER of my LORD and SAVIOR JESUS CHRIST, to Baptize me now with YOUR HOLY GHOST and Power.

YOUR WORD in Matthew 28:19-20, says, YOU have all POWER. You said that, I am to go therefore, and teach all nations, baptizing and teaching them to observe, the work of YOU FATHER, SON and HOLY GHOST. Thereby, properly discipling them in what the Doctrine of CHRIST, that is found in Hebrews 6:1-2 are. This is so that they may go on unto perfection. This I know will lay a solid foundation upon which they can build their Spiritual House in CHRIST JESUS the LORD'S Name. You said, without YOU, I can do nothing but that I can do all things through CHRIST WHICH STRENGHTENS ME. FATHER, I Receive YOUR HOLY SPIRIT, HIS POWER in order to also be YOUR Witness and Ambassador, in this world.

I expect to speak in tongues now, as YOUR SPIRIT gives me utterance, IN CHRIST JESUS my LORDS NAME. Thank YOU. HOLY SPIRIT, I acknowledge YOU, and YOU do direct my path. Thank YOU for the Grace, to Live in the SPIRIT, walk in the SPIRIT, be led by the SPIRIT, and manifest the Fruit of the SPIRIT always. I ask for all of this, and receive it now, in JESUS CHRIST my LORD'S name by HOLY GHOST Orchestration, and the Covenant that is sealed in the Blood of JESUS, YESHUA, The CHRIST's name and for YOUR Glory and Honor ABBA FATHER! I Confess, CHRIST in me the Hope of Glory!!!

QUESTION & ANSWER WORKSHEET

1. List the Six Foundation Stones found in Hebrews 6:1-2

_____
_____
_____
_____
_____

2. Summarized each of The First Three Foundation Stones found in Hebrews 6:1-2.

_____
_____
_____
_____
_____
_____
_____
_____
_____
_____
_____
_____
_____
_____
_____
_____
_____

Encouraging, Empowering, and Equipping the Church for Execution...
The Next Move
 ## THE GREAT AWAKENING!
ROOTED AND GROUNDED IN THE FAITH

The Remaining Three Foundational Stones are so IMPORTANT too! Number Four, "**THE LAYING ON OF HANDS**, Five "**THE RESURRECTION FOR THE DEAD**" and Six "**ETERNAL JUDGMENT**." What are they all about? The teaching on how many Resurrections are there? Along with Rewards, Crowns and where will the Believers go for Judgment and where will the Unbelievers go for their judgment? On what will they be judged? Each one of these Stones would make this teaching an additional 3 or 4 pages. Therefore, I pray to have another opportunity to pick back up on these Essential Foundational Stones. I desire to have all Six Foundational Stones Laid Properly in everyone's life. That all will be Equipped, Rooted and Grounded on a Solid Foundation upon which to build their Faith. All becoming Bolder Disciples, ready and willing to defend the Gospel and Properly Disciple others. Let's continue. Remember the WORD says, better is the end of a thing than the beginning. Let's GO!!!

HOLY SPIRIT'S EQUIPPING ALL BELIEVERS... AND YOURSELF!!!
PART II

In Part One, you were asked: How EQUIPPED ARE YOU? This question was not intended to embarrass, condemn nor to intimidate you or anyone. But on the contrary. The question is asked only to awaken you to your own Spiritual Pulse or Spiritual Condition. There is No Condemnation. However, the question remains: How Strong Is Your Spiritual Foundation? Have you personally understood, experienced, and learned what, being Rooted and Grounded in your Faith is Truly All About? In Part One of this book, we went over the First Three Foundation Stones found in Hebrews 6:1-2. However, it is essential that you know and understand all Six of The Foundation Stones. As a natural house or building, without a solid foundation is going to encounter trouble, so is your spiritual house if, its foundation is not properly laid. You too would be headed for problems.

JESUS gave the Parable of the Wise and the Foolish Builders in Matthew 7:24-27. In summary of this very familiar Parable, you are told to Build Your House on the ROCK. Right? Right. Very Good.

The Bible, the WORD of GOD seems to believe that a Solid Christian Foundation, is SO.... IMPORTANT, that there are approximately 100 Scripture References on it. Review the passages of Scriptures in Luke 6:47-49, and in 1 Corinthians 3:13-16 for just a couple of them.

As a brief review from Part One, what are the Six Foundation Stones, upon which each Spiritual House is to be built upon?
HEBREWS 6:1-2. "Now leaving the Principles of the Doctrine of CHRIST, let us go on unto Perfection. Not Laying again the foundations of:

1. REPENTANCE FROM DEAD WORKS
2. FAITH TOWARD GOD
3. DOCTRINE OF BAPTISMS
4. LAYING ON OF HANDS
5. RESURRECTION OF THE DEAD
6. ETERNAL JUDGEMENT

…And this will we do if GOD Permits."

GOD is permitting this because, there is a Need!

Let's go on to address the remaining Three (3) Foundation Stones. Please, do your part, even if you feel you already know and understand the Six Stones; review them and let this be the standard by which you disciple others. The goal of the FATHER, is that you be properly discipled and then, go make disciples. Again, we will be using the Doctrines found in Hebrews 6:1-2. All Six of the Foundational Stones Are Equally IMPORTANT!

Foundation Stone Four: The Doctrine of
"LAYING ON OF HANDS" (Hebrews 6:2a)

LAYING ON OF HANDS is a Biblical Doctrine that is repeatedly seen in Scripture to denote impartation, consecration and/or dedication. The Right Hand is to be used during this service, etc. Again, Laying Hands should be with the Right Hand (The hand of favor and anointing), Revelation 1:17.

As with the Right Side, the Right Hand is always identified as GOD's Special Place or Status of Favor, Honor and Strength. The Right Hand is mentioned in a favorable and positive way, over 100 times in the Holy Bible. Whereas the left hand is referenced 25 times in Scripture and all in a negative or unfavorable light.

A couple of Old Testament Biblical examples of the "Right Hand" are found in Exodus 15:6 and Psalm 118:16. Both Scriptures do mention that the Right Hand is the Hand of Strength. Also, remember where JESUS CHRIST our LORD sat, after HE was obedient unto death, even the death on the Cross. "And being found in fashion as a man, HE humbled HIMSELF, and became obedient unto death, even the death of the cross. Wherefore GOD also hath highly exalted HIM and given HIM a Name which is above every name," (Phil. 2:8-9). Where does JESUS sit? You are correct. The LORD JESUS CHRIST sits at the Right Hand of the FATHER. The place of Highest Honor, Favor, and Equal Status, with GOD the FATHER. HE, JESUS is within the GODHEAD.

I'm taking a little sidebar or rabbit trail. Getting slightly off subject here: When you present in Worship, your Tithes to the LORD, please remember to place it in your Right Hand. This shows that you have consecrated your first ten percent as unto the LORD. You are bringing to HIM what is Right and not, what is left. You are not giving HIM your Tithes, because it already belongs to HIM. Therefore, you are bringing the LORD, what is HIS, (Mal. 3:10) and this keeps you from being a GOD robber. Amen? Amen!

Very Good answer. Your Offering is what you give. It is over and beyond the 10% Tithe. It can be of any amount. But remember, with what measure you sow, it will be measured back to you.

Back on track. We are taught not to Lay Hands Suddenly on any one or thing for that matter, (I Timothy 5:22). Wait until you sense a release of your faith and or the Unction from HOLY SPIRIT; then release the Power by the Laying on of your Right Hand on the person/persons, etc.

In many places in Scripture, there is the **LAYING ON OF HANDS** accompanied with the Anointing with Oil.

SELF-QUIZ:

1. When anointing with oil, the power of GOD is in the oil.
True _____
False _____

2. Jesus' disciples used the unusual ministry of anointing with oil with many that were sick and healed them.
True _____
False _____

3. Anointing with oil is not for deliverance to the oppressed.
True _____
False _____

(Answers: 1. F 2. T 3. F)

~David mentioned this special anointing with Oil when writing Psalm 23.

~James 5:14-15 tells us to do 3 things for the sick to be healed:

a. "let him call for the elders of the Church.
b. and let them pray over him.
c. anointing him with oil in the name of the LORD.

Results: "And the Prayer of Faith shall heal the sick, and The LORD shall raise him up: and if he has committed sins, they shall be forgiven him."

The Oil alone has no power. However, when saturated by prayer & faith, the Oil becomes a point of contact. Holy Spirit's point of power for bringing deliverance to people. If the Anointing is present, something is going to Happen. The Anointing is JESUS' BURDEN REMOVING, YOKE DESTROYING POWER OF GOD at work. The Oil Is referenced as a type of GOD, The HOLY SPIRIT.

A few Instances where:

~Jesus Lays Hands: Luke 5:13 and Matt. 19:15
~The Apostles Lay Hands: Acts 6:6

Several Reasons and or Occasions that Hands were laid:

1. Laying on of Hands for Healing and Casting Out devils Luke 4:40
2. Laying Hands to Bless Children Mark 10:16
3. Laying Hands for Imparting Blessing to next generation Genesis 48:14
4. Laying Hands to Heal after Praying Acts 28:8
6. Laying Hands for Commission and Ordination Acts 13:2-3
7. Laying Hands before Stoning Leviticus 24:14
8. Laying Hands following Fasting and Praying Acts 13:3
9. Laying Hands for Impartation of Spiritual Gifts 1 Timothy 4:14
10. Laying Hands for Saints to Receive Infilling of HOLY SPIRIT Acts 8:17

Foundation Stone Five Doctrine of
"THE RESURRECTION OF THE DEAD" (Hebrews 6:2b)

Meaning of Resurrection: Rising from death.

The difference between the FOUR TYPES of Resurrections:

~People Raised from death back to life.
~The Resurrection of CHRIST JESUS
~Dead Believers in CHRIST JESUS the LORD, Resurrected and
~The Resurrection of the Just and Unjust

Throughout the Scriptures, in both the Old & New Testament:

People were bought back to life after being dead.
People Raised back to Life:

Old Testament Examples:

Widow's son, 1 Kings 17:17-22

Shunammite's Son, 2 Kings 4:32-35

Unnamed man, 2 Kings 13:20-21

New Testament Examples:

Jarius' daughter, Matthew 9:23-25,

Widow's only son, Luke 7:11-15

Lazarus John 11:43-44, Many Saints, Matthews 27:52-53

Dorcas Acts 9:36-40

There are also several accounts of people being raised back to life from death today. The people that died in both the Old and New Testament accounts, died again at some time and point. Their bodies are still in the grave. But not so with the LORD JESUS. In that HE died, HE died unto sin once and HE LIVES FOREVER! (Romans 6:10 KJV)

Why is it so important to know that JESUS CHRIST, The LORD did Resurrect from death? Well, because without it we, as Born-Again Believers in CHRIST JESUS would be of most people miserable. If our SAVIOR JESUS had died and remain dead then, HE has no power to do anything for us. We would be miserable because HE would not be able to deliver us from our sin debt, after this life ends. We would only have awaiting us: death, hell the grave which is Eternal Separation from GOD. Yes, Eternal damnation in hell would be our portion throughout all of eternity. Not Good! Miserable!

BUT!!!!! CONJUNCTION!!! KING JESUS our LORD and CHRIST, yes, HE resurrected on the third day following HIS crucifixion for our Sins! He Arose with All Power Over Satan, Sin, Death, Hell, and the Grave.

THE RESURRECTION OF THE JUST AND UNJUST

First - The Just...

Additionally, for those Born-Again Believers (The Just), that have already died, being absent from their bodies, they are present with the LORD. Remember they are absent from their bodies. The body of the saved believer gets separated from their spirit and soul when they experience physical death. The spirit and soul of the believer that died knowing JESUS as their LORD and SAVIOR, did not die; it is present with the LORD. However, on the day, which the Bible speaks of as the "Taken Away or Catching Away, Caught Up," in the Greek language known as the "Rapture" of the Church, the Physical bodies of the dead saints, born again believers will be resurrected from death and rejoined with their spirit and soul in a glorified body. A body that will never die again, (1 Thessalonians 4:16-18, 2 Corinthians 5:1-10). Following, please see two translations: the King James Version and the New King James Version of the Bible's account of these events...

[16]"For the LORD HIMSELF shall descend from heaven with a shout, with the voice of the archangel, and with the trump of GOD: and the dead in Christ shall rise first: [17]Then we which are alive and remain shall be caught up together with them in the clouds, to meet the LORD in the air: and so shall we ever be with the LORD. [18]Wherefore comfort one another with these words."
1 Thessalonians 4:16-18 KJV

"[14]For if we believe that JESUS died and rose again, even so GOD will bring with HIM those who sleep in JESUS. (Sleep as in death) [15]For this we say to you by the WORD of the LORD, that we who are alive and remain until the coming of the LORD will by no

means precede those who are asleep. ¹⁶For the LORD HIMSELF will descend from heaven with a shout, with the voice of an archangel, and with the trumpet of GOD. And the dead in CHRIST will rise first. (Resurrect first) ¹⁷Then we who are alive and remain shall be caught up together with them in the clouds to meet the LORD in the air. And thus, we shall always be with the LORD. ¹⁸Therefore comfort one another with these words."
1 Thessalonians 4:14-18 NKJ

In summary, the dead in CHRIST JESUS will rise- resurrect-first. Then, we who are still alive will be caught up with them in the clouds. We will all be changed and given glorified bodies with no flesh and blood. Life will be which will never die. Our hope is in the truth that we know we have been forgiven and will not be damned to hell, separated from GOD. We have Eternal Life through and by our LORD JESUS CHRIST.

On the third day, JESUS CHRIST was resurrected by FATHER GOD with a glorified body. HE will never, ever die again. HE lives forever! This gives hope for those that have loved ones, that have died in the LORD; (died being a Born-Again Believer). This is the hope of those of us who will remain alive until the coming of The LORD JESUS CHRIST for HIS Church in the Rapture. **Hallelujah x 7!**

Because JESUS was resurrected with a body that will never die again, every believer has the same promise given them by Our LORD. We have the hope and the assurance of a glorified body that will live forever. The Scriptures foretells of all believers, whether alive or if they have fallen asleep in death, all of us will be changed. A new body which is described as a glorified body that will never die; be sickly, or age. This is what will be given to us. Our glorified bodies will not consist of flesh and blood. Why? Because flesh and human blood will not enter the kingdom of GOD. The body with flesh and human blood are corruptible (can decay and die). Only what is incorruptible (will not decay or die) will inherit or enter into GOD's Heaven.

> "Now this I say, brethren, that flesh and blood cannot inherit the kingdom of God; neither doth corruption inherit incorruption."
> Corinthians 15:50

All Born Again Christians, (The Just, those that have been justified, forgiven of their sins, washed in the Blood of JESUS and by grace through faith are saved) will receive glorified bodies and enjoy eternal life with the LORD forever. (Ephesians 2:8-9)

At the Rapture, the believer's body will be changed. It will be just like the LORD JESUS' body when HE resurrected on that third day. What was some of the things that JESUS did after He Resurrected? HE could move about at the speed of thought. HE appeared in a room with both doors and windows locked, (John 20:26). HE ate food, HE was recognizable and able to recognize and communicate with the disciples. Yes, all true believers will be changed, and we will see HIM as HE is and we will be just like HIM.

> "Beloved, now are we the sons of GOD and it doeth not yet appear what we shall be; but we know that, when HE shall appear, we shall be like HIM: for we shall see HIM as HE is. Everyone that have this hope purifies himself even as HE (JESUS) is Pure."
> 1 John 3:2-3

THE RESURRECTION OF THE UNJUST...

Remember, there is a resurrection of the Just but also of the Unjust. John 5:29: "And shall come forth, they that have done good, unto the resurrection of life; and they that have done evil, unto the resurrection of damnation (Judgment)."

In John 5:28-30, JESUS says...
"Do not be amazed at this, for a time is coming when all who are in their graves will hear HIS voice [29]and come out—those who have done what is good will rise to live, and those who have done what is evil will rise to be condemned. [30]By myself I can do nothing; I judge only as I hear, and my judgment is just, for I seek not to please myself but him who sent me."

Those that died, without seeing a need to accept JESUS CHRIST as their own personal SAVIOR and LORD, will have to pay the wages of their own sins. (Romans 6:23).

JESUS died so that whosoever, that is anyone and everyone, could be saved through HIM. However, GOD created each of us with a free will. We have a free will to accept or reject.

HE does not want robots that are forced to choose HIM. This is a love relationship that HE offers to all who would believe and trust their lives to HIM. Satan seeks to force his evil will and plans on people in order to steal, kill and destroy them. But not GOD. LOVE sent JESUS to the Cross to die for all and GOD is LOVE. (1 John 4:8.)

The LORD GOD said in Deuteronomy 30:19, "Today I have given you the choice between life and death, between blessings and curses. Now I call on heaven and earth to witness the choice you make. Oh, that you would choose life, so that you and your descendants might live!"

"The Spirit and the bride say, "Come." Let anyone who hears this say, "Come." Let anyone who is thirsty come. Let anyone who desires drink freely from the water of life."
Revelation 22:17

JESUS Paid It All! GOD sent JESUS that the world through HIM might be saved.

JESUS became a curse for us so that we could be blessed. FATHER GOD gave HIS ONLY BEGOTTEN SON (JESUS), that whosoever would believe on HIM would not perish but have everlasting life. JESUS said, whosoever believes and is baptized will be saved, but whoever does not believe will be damned or condemned to eternal separation from GOD. As you see, just like the Just, the Unjust choose their own eternal destination. Punishment for their sins is, death, hell and then hell is thrown into the lake of fire, Read: Galatians 3:13, John 3:16-17, Mark 16:16, and Revelation 20:10-15.

The resurrection of the Unjust dead will be further explained in the final Foundation Stone, Eternal Judgment.

However, if you are not sure if you are the Just or the Unjust, then now is the time. Today is the day to make that decision. Through repentance and acceptance of the LORD JESUS CHRIST's sacrifice for your sins, you can become Born Again, Saved, A Believer, or the Just (meaning, Justified and made right with GOD in and by CHRIST JESUS). If you need to rededicate your life to GOD through CHRIST JESUS, this is the time to do so. Also: Whosoever will, let HIM come to JESUS and be Saved! Romans 3:23 says, that "For all have sinned and come short of the glory of GOD." Romans 6:23 says, "The wages (payment) for sin is death, (total separation from GOD) but, the gift of GOD is eternal life through JESUS CHRIST the LORD."

Romans 10:13 says, "Whosoever, (that's anyone), shall call upon the Name of the LORD, shall be saved." (From their sins, death, hell, and eternal separation from GOD forever).

If you would like to make sure that you are forgiven of your sins and have eternal life then, here is a suggested prayer that you can pray out loud Now. Today is the Day of Salvation…

PRAY:

GOD, I confess out loud with my mouth, that I have sinned, and I have come short of YOUR glory GOD. I repent of my sins (turning away from them), I ask your forgiveness. I accept your gift of eternal life through JESUS CHRIST the LORD. JESUS CHRIST is LORD and I confess this with my own mouth. JESUS died for my sins, shedding all of HIS blood to cleanse me of them. I believe that HE was buried, but that HE rose from the dead on the third day, according to the Scriptures. I confess with my mouth the LORD JESUS and I believe in my heart that YOU GOD raised JESUS from the dead. Now according to YOUR WORD, I am saved, born again. I am **now** a believe, that is Just; Justified made righteous (in right standing) with YOU GOD as my HEAVENLY FATHER right **now**, through JESUS CHRIST my LORD and SAVIOR. Thank YOU, LORD JESUS, for saving me! (Romans 10:9-10, Acts 2:38, Ephesians 2:8-9)

Well, **Hallelujah x 7!** The angels in heaven are rejoicing over you, (Luke 15:10).

Also, your name, just got written down in the LAMB's Book of Life, (Revelation 21:27). Hallelujah!

<u>STEPS TO TAKE ONCE SAVED...</u>

You are <u>**Baptized into the Family of GOD Now**</u>! Yes, HE is your HEAVENLY FATHER.

1. Unite with a Bible Believing, Teaching and Doing Ministry (Church). Pray, ask the LORD to lead you to where HE would plant you in HIS Church, the Body of CHRIST. Also, should you desire help with finding a WORD, SPIRIT Filled, Bible Believing Ministry / Church, in your area. Also, feel free to:

<u>**Email:**</u> loretta.rich@outlook.com
<u>**Write:**</u> P.O. BOX 783
Clinton, Maryland 20735

2. Next, following the Apostles of the LORD JESUS CHRIST throughout the Book of Acts, as soon as possible <u>**you must get Baptized in Water in JESUS NAME. That is unless there is a really GOOD reason(s) that prohibits you from doing so**</u>.

Remember, and even review, if necessary, <u>Foundation Stone Three</u>: <u>THE DOCTRINE OF BAPTISMS</u> that is covered in this Book.

3. Receive the **Baptism of HOLY SPIRIT as well.** I suggest that you start over again reading this Book, but this time as a New Believer in CHRIST. By reviewing you will be assured that you are properly discipled, rooted and grounded in the faith and being given a **solid foundation** upon which to build your Spiritual House. Welcome, Welcome, Welcome!

Please Share!

Text or Call: (240) 435-9293
Write: P.O. Box 783 Clinton, Md 20735
Email: loretta.rich@outlook.com

Share your name, when you got born again or, when you rededicated your life to CHRIST as SAVIOR and LORD. Feel free to also visit the website: www.weightaside.org.

For prayer or to get other copy(s) of the Rooted and Grounded Bootcamp Book/Manual so that you can get to work helping others to get properly discipled then like you, they can later make disciples Obeying JESUS' Command (Matthew 28:19). Please use the same number to Text or Call, Email Address or Write to the P.O. Box listed above.

Now, just before we begin our Six and final Foundation Stone that is found in Hebrews 6:1-2, you can rejoice because Eternal Judgment will be a blessing for you.

WORKSHEET

Review Questions & Please Answer
(Refer back to the Lesson when needed.)

1. Is the Laying on of hands Biblical for the New Testament Church?
Yes   _____
No   _____

2. List three reasons from the Bible for laying hands.
_____
_____
_____
_____

3. List the things that should be considered when Laying Hands?
_____
_____
_____
_____

4. Can Oil be used when Laying Hands?
Yes   _____
No   _____

If so, what type of oil should be used, and should there be any preparation prior to using the oil? Explain your answer.
_____
_____
_____

5. GOD, by HIS SPIRIT in JESUS' names Heals in many ways. Using James 5:14, list the steps that are to be taken in this type of Healing.

_____
_____
_____
_____

6. Can you only Anoint and Lay Hands on people?
Yes _____
No   _____

Explain your answer.

_____
_____
_____
_____

7. Summarize the Four Types of Resurrections:

_____
_____
_____
_____
_____
_____
_____
_____
_____
_____

Sixth Foundation Stone: "THE DOCTRINE OF ETERNAL JUDGMENT"

There are two places where GOD's Judgment will take place. One place is called the **Judgment Seat of CHRIST**, and the other is called The Great White Throne Judgment. One Judgment place is for the Born-Again Believer and the other place is for the Unsaved, Un-repented, Undegenerated Sinner. Guess who goes where? You are correct, the Judgment Seat of CHRIST. That is where the believer; the Just will appear before their SAVIOR, JESUS CHRIST. In contrast, **The Great White Throne Judgment** is where the Unbeliever, the Unjust; those that rejected CHRIST will appear before GOD to be judged. They must pay for their own sins. Remember, Romans 6:23, "For the wages of sin is death, but the gift of GOD (that they rejected during their lifetime here on planet earth), is Eternal Life through JESUS CHRIST our LORD."

When is it Eternal Judgment Time? Well first, for those that are currently deceased. Those that will die prior to the Rapture if, during their lifetime here on planet earth, they did believe and accepted the LORD JESUS CHRIST'S Blood as Payment and Cleansing of their sins. They believed in HIS bodily resurrection from the dead which justified them; before a HOLY GOD; (WHO cannot look on sin), (as you learned in our study of the Fifth Foundation Stone), they will be resurrected back to life. They will receive a body that will never die again, a glorified body. They will be caught up to meet the LORD JESUS CHRIST in the air and forever be with HIM.

Second, the believers that are alive and remain when the Rapture occurs will be changed and also given a glorified body. They too will be caught up in the clouds to meet the LORD in the air. Both will be taken to heaven, (1 Thessalonians 4:14-17). For them, Eternal Judgment will take place in Heaven. Yes, it's time for their judgment. They will all, individually appear before what is called The Judgment Seat of CHRIST; also known as the Bema Seat of CHRIST. 2 Corinthians 5:10, KJV, "For we must all (Believers) appear before the **Judgment Seat of CHRIST** that everyone may receive the things done in his body, according to that he hath done, whether it be good or bad." The Sinner and unbeliever will not be there. Only those that have believed on the LORD JESUS CHRIST: HIS death, burial, resurrection from the dead, repented of their sins, received forgiveness, and have been washed and cleansed in the Blood of JESUS. This judgement is for those that have turned their lives over to JESUS and now will appear before HIM. The true Christians will not be judged for their sins because, "**JESUS Paid It All, All To HIM I (They) Owe; Sin had left A Crimson Stain- HE Washed It White As Snow**," (as the Hymn by Elvina M Hall and John T Grape wrote).

In summary, JESUS CHRIST the LORD became the Holy Sin Sacrifice by dying on the Cross to remove their sin debt. Once a Christian is Born Again, they enter into a Blood Covenant with GOD through CHRIST JESUS. **Again, all of their sins are forgiven. They have access to the Blessings of GOD through JESUS CHRIST their LORD.**

However, once saved, the Baptized Born-Again Believers is expected to do good works. Works that will glorify GOD their HEAVENLY FATHER. Yes, after they have given their lives to GOD through CHRIST, they are expected as a family member in the family of GOD, to do their chores, Lol.

Quick Review: Remember, as you learned JESUS and every Born-Again Believer **must** have all **three DOCTRINES OF BAPTISMS** as an experienced / reality in their life.

1.) Being Birthed by the SPIRIT, with the believer Baptized into the Family of GOD, 2.) Baptized (Immersed) in Water in JESUS Name, and 3.) Baptized with HOLY SPIRIT.

All of the Baptisms are to be **prior** to working for GOD! JESUS HIMSELF had to be empowered by HOLY GHOST, then HIS earthy Ministry started. HE continued until it was, as HE said: "IT IS FINISHED!" Yes, because of CHRIST JESUS, our **Great Example Setter,** doing everything decently and in the FATHER GOD'S order, believers benefit now and for all of eternity. Hallelujah!

It is right there during their Eternal Judgement, at the Judgment Seat of CHRIST their LORD that their work(s) will get judged. Their works will matter and count if, the works were done with the correct / right motives. Born Again Spirit Filled Christians are expected to work with and through the Power of HOLY GHOST to serve the LORD in CHRIST JESUS their SAVIOR's Name. (Acts, 1:8, Ephesians 4:11-16, 1 Corinthians 12:11-31, John 9:4).

They appear before the Judgement Seat of CHRIST, as opposed to, **The Great White Throne Judgment),** Where the Rejecters of CHRIST will appear for their Eternal Judgement Sentence, (Teaching coming up in this Section).

Believers must follow their LORD's example which is to, "Work while it was day, lest, night come, and no man can work." Believers were to have been about fulfilling GOD'S purpose for them. JESUS understood this when HE was here on planet earth. HE told HIS parents, didn't they know, that HE would be about HIS FATHER's business. JESUS was only 12 years old when HE said that. JESUS knew HIS purpose back then but, HE had to wait 18 more years to truly begin, and walk HIS purpose out.

In light of the LORD JESUS CHRIST finishing HIS course, we are able to be forgiven, saved, and Eternally Blessed. I am asking you, JESUS' Disciple, "**Who is depending on you fulfilling and completing the work that the LORD has set apart for you to do** and if they receive it, they will benefit from your labor, for all of eternity too. JESUS said, The Greater Works shall you do, (HIS Body of Believers do), because HE has gone to the FATHER.

Who could be saved and Properly Discipled, if you, for an example, obeyed the Great Commission; which is to "**Go make disciples**…"? The race isn't given to the swift, nor to the strong but to him that will endure to the end, the scripture states.

For those of us, that have been working with HOLY SPIRIT to fulfill what the FATHER has set for us to do, I pray that we will by HOLY SPIRIT'S GRACE will not become weary in doing well; for we shall reap in this life, and at Eternal Judgment. If we faint not. GOD Sees and Rewards.

The body of CHRIST consists of many members and each one has to do their part now. The race to finish well has already begun. Don't try and run someone else's race. You will only get rewarded for finishing the work / race that the LORD has assigned for you to do while you are here on planet earth.

Remember JESUS taught on "The Parable of the Talents" in Matthew 25:14-30? (NKJV),

> [14]"For the kingdom of heaven is like a man traveling to a far country, who called his own servants and delivered his goods to them. [15]And to one he gave five talents, to another two, and to another one, to each according to his own ability; and immediately he went on a journey. [16]Then he who had received the five talents went and traded with them and made another five talents. [17]And likewise he who had received two gained two more also. [18]But he who had received one went and dug in the ground and hid his lord's money. [19]After a long time the lord of those servants came and settled accounts with them. [20]"So he who had received five talents came and brought five other talents, saying, 'Lord, you delivered to me five talents; look, I have gained five more talents besides them. [21]His lord said to him, 'Well done, good and faithful servant; you were faithful over a few things, I will make you ruler over many things. Enter into the joy of your lord. [22]He also who had received two talents came and said, 'Lord, you delivered to me two talents; look, I have gained two more talents besides them. [23]His lord said to him, Well done, good and faithful servant; you have been faithful over a few things, I will make you ruler over many things. Enter into the joy of your lord. [24]"Then he who had received the one talent came and said, 'Lord, I knew you to be a hard man, reaping where you have not sown, and gathering where you have not scattered seed. [25]And I was afraid and went and hid your talent in the ground. Look, there you have what is yours.' [26]"But his lord answered and said to him, 'You wicked and lazy servant, you knew that I reap

where I have not sown and gather where I have not scattered seed. ²⁷So you ought to have deposited my money with the bankers, and on my coming I would have received back my own with interest. ²⁸So take the talent from him and give it to him who has ten talents. ²⁹'For to everyone who has, more will be given, and he will have abundance; but from him who does not have, even what he has will be taken away. ³⁰And cast the unprofitable servant into the outer darkness. There will be weeping and gnashing of teeth.'

JESUS is the man that goes away to a far country, (HE went back to Heaven). We know HE will return. The believers are HIS servants that HE has given talents and gifts to. HE expects them to use the talents and gifts that HE gave them. HE expects them to get to work. And to complete what HE had started. JESUS has given each Christian gifts and talents. When HE returns to get HIS Church, HE does expect an increase from what HE has given. The unprofitable servant in the Parable, buried the talent and produced nothing. The servant was a very bad example and HE wasted time and the talent. You do not want to be anything like that servant because remember, at the Judgment Seat of CHRIST, there will be rewards or lack of rewards. An account will be given of the believer's stewardship of what they have been given. If you are not sure, just ask HOLY SPIRIT what should you be doing and what gifts and talents have HE given to you? Then get busy fulfilling a need and as you serve, then your gifts will make room for you, as the scripture says, (Proverbs 18:16).

If the work(s) that are done glorified GOD and was done with the right motives, then it is considered a good work. Jesus will judge the works of what sort they were. Again, the children of GOD must all appear at the Judgment Seat of CHRIST (Bema Seat). There is where each individual's works will be judged; deeds that were done in their body. All rewards will be determined by JESUS CHRIST, The LORD HIMSELF.

There are Six Categories or types of works that a Born-Again child of GOD can produce namely: 1. Gold 2. Silver 3. Precious Stones 4. Wood 5. Hay 6. Stubble

> [12] " Now, if any man builds upon this foundation gold, silver, precious stones, wood, hay, stubble; [13] Every man's work shall be made manifest: for the day shall declare it, because it shall be revealed by fire; and the fire shall try every man's work of what sort it is."
> 1 Corinthians 3:12-13

We are told that the works "shall be revealed by fire." What happens when fire is put to Gold, Silver, and Precious Stones? You are correct. It becomes even more pure.

What happens when fire is put to Wood, Hay or Stubble? You are right again. It gets burned up. Therefore, the good works that the believers do will be classified as either gold, silver, or precious stones. These works will become even more valuable as they are treasures that the believers have set up in heaven, (Matthew 6:19-20). The bad works will be wood, hay or stubble. These works will be burned up. I know you wouldn't want any of your works to get burned up. You would desire to have more good works, treasures than bad works. Therefore, while there is still time, get busy fulfilling the purpose for which you alone can produce. Thank GOD for the grace to repent now of the bad works and go forth.

Remember, Matthew 6:19-20 says, [19]" Lay not up for yourselves treasures upon earth, where moth and rust doth corrupt, and where thieves break through and steal: [20]But lay up for yourselves treasures in heaven, where neither moth nor rust doth corrupt, and where thieves do not break through nor steal."

Since we are told that the works; good and bad shall be revealed by fire then, years ago, I wanted to know just where would this fire, that would judge the believer's works come from? I asked HOLY SPIRIT and I believe that HE gave me the answer. I believe, I was led to look at the physical appearance of The LORD JESUS CHRIST as described in Revelation 2:18. It states… "And unto the angel of the church in Thyatira write, these things saith the SON of GOD, WHO hath HIS eyes like unto a flame of fire, and HIS feet are like fine brass;" Also, Revelation 19:12, "HIS eyes were as a flame of fire, and on HIS head were many crowns; and HE had a name written, that no man knew, but HE HIMSELF."

> "HIS head and HIS hairs were white like wool, as white as snow; and HIS eyes were as a flame of fire;"
> Revelation 1:14

We know that JESUS' eyes that are like a flame of fire did look seriously, and earnestly as HE examined the seven churches. HE told five of the churches what pleased HIM. But HE still had something against them. HE told them what it was and then gave them space to repent in. JESUS told them to get things right, or HE would remove their candlestick. JESUS also saw through HIS own eyes which, are as a flame of fire that two of the churches had stayed the course. HE encouraged them to continue in what they were doing. HE told them that HE wanted them to continue being steadfast, and unmovable, always abounding in the work of the LORD, forasmuch as they know that their labor is not in vain in the LORD, (1 Corinthians 15:18).

At the Judgment Seat of CHRIST, I truly believe that the same LORD JESUS WHOM, with HIS HOLY, Pure, without sin and guile eyes, which are as a flame of fire that examined the Churches in the Book of Revelation, will also judge the believer's works. JESUS can only see what is true. Therefore, HE will truly know of what sort the works are. Believers are told that the works of the Church, (the believer's works), "shall be revealed by fire."

Even in the Old Testament we see that judgement is done by the LORD, WHOM HIMSELF is as a FIRE. (Malachi 3:2-3 King James Version of the Holy Bible), But who shall abide the day of HIS coming? And who shall stand when HE appeareth? HE is like a REFINER's FIRE and like FULLER'S SOAP. And HE shall sit as a REFINER and PURIFIER of silver: and HE shall purify the sons of Levi, and purge them as gold and silver, that they may offer unto the LORD and offering in righteousness." Malachi 3:6 further says, "For I AM The LORD I change not therefore you sons of Jacob are not consumed."

(The New Living Translation's Version of Malachi 3:2), "But who will be able to stand and face HIM when HE appears? For HE will be like a BLAZING FIRE that refines metal or like a STRONG SOAP that whitens clothes. "HE will sit and judge like a REFINER of silver, watching closely as the dross is burned away. HE will purify the Levites, refining them like gold or silver, so that they may once again offer acceptable sacrifices to the LORD." Malachi 3:6

further says, "I AM The LORD, and I do not change. That is why you descendants of Jacob are not already completely destroyed."

As we know, the Old Testament Levitical Priest that, GOD HIMSELF set apart, did not have the Blood of JESUS CHRIST to save, cleanse and take away their sins. JESUS CHRIST THE LORD, had not come into the world to die for sinners yet. Therefore, GOD had to sit as JUDGE, A REFINER's FIRE and like a STRONG SOAP to temporarily purify the Priest. However, the New Testament Scriptures, makes it very clear that, JESUS is EMMANUEL, GOD WITH US! Therefore, <u>ONLY</u> through HIS Blood SACRIFICED on the CROSS, can all mankind be saved, cleansed, born again, quickened (made alive, by GOD's HOLY SPIRIT), redeemed, and made a partaker of eternal life through accepting JEUS CHRIST as LORD and SAVIOR Hallelujah!

The LORD said, "<u>I do not change</u>." Therefore, if HE, being the FIRE that judged, refined and purified the Priest that HE selected in the Old Testament then, it will be CHRIST JESUS The LORD, WHO by HOLY GHOST Orchestration, I strongly believe, revealed this to me. HE will judge with HIS Own Pure Eyes of Fire, HIS Own Church; the Body of CHRIST for which HE Sacrificed and died! Most parents desire to correct and reward their own child/children, sometimes by just, giving them that "Eye." Just a thought.

What do you think?
Yes ___
No ___
Maybe ___

Further Scripture References:
Isaiah 60:7b, "I will glorify the house of MY Glory!"

John 5:21-23, JESUS said: "For as the FATHER raiseth up the dead, and quickeneth (makes alive) them; even so the SON quickeneth whom HE will. For the FATHER (ABBA GOD now, that CHRIST the SON is SAVIOR), JUDGETH No Man, but hath committed all judgement unto the SON. That all men should honor the SON, even as they honor the FATHER."

John 5:26-27, "For as the FATHER hath life in HIMSELF; so hath HE given to the SON (JESUS) to have life in HIMSELF. And hath given HIM (JESUS) authority to execute judgment also, because HE is the SON OF MAN."

At the Judgment Seat of CHRIST, the Church of JESUS must never forget that all of their deeds that were done in their bodies, rather good or bad will be judged. All of the works will be determined by JESUS WHO is The HEAD of HIS Church. HE will know if the believer's deeds are classified as gold, silver, precious stone, wood, hay, or stubble.

Like the Churches in the Book of Revelation, believers have been given space to repent, turn from the things that are not right. All believers right now can, lay aside every weight and the sins that so easily beset them and to run the race that is set before them, looking unto JESUS the AUTHOR and FINISHER of their faith. (Hebrews 12:1-2).

All have another opportunity to work, the works of CHRIST while it is day lest, night come, and no man can work. A strong

Admonition... Like the wise virgins be ready. Let your light shine before men, that they may see your good works, and glorify your FATHER which is in Heaven. Work as unto the LORD and not as unto men, knowing that of the LORD you will receive your rewards. (John 9:4, Matthew 25:1-13, Matt. 5:16, Colossians 3:23) Some Christians believe that all they want to do is make it into heaven. Some don't care about receiving rewards for good deeds. However, remember in grade school and beyond when the Award Assemblies were held? How you felt if your name wasn't called in any of the categories to receive an award? No, not even for Physical Education. That was not a very good feeling, was it? Look you didn't have to work to get save and into the family of GOD.

The LORD JESUS took care of all of your sin debt and punishments. Therefore, in light of that you should rejoice at the opportunity to serve and fulfill your GOD given purpose from the heart. Remember once Born Again, your works, no matter how great or small in your eyes will matter at the Judgment Seat of CHRIST. So, as a faithful family member in the Body of CHRIST, GET YOUR CHORES DONE. In the end, you will be glad you did.

Review: Again, Remember the Crowns...
At the Judgment Seat of CHRIST there are more rewards. Five Crowns are to be given to those that have earned them. The Greek word for Crown is Stephanes. The root for the name Stephen. Stephen in the Book of Acts was martyred. The name itself means a badge of honor, badge of loyalty, prize for winning a contest. Crown is the word used in the New Testament to speak of rewards that GOD promises to give those who are faithful. First Corinthians 9:24-25 speaks of the Crowns that all believers can receive if they are in the race. Each believer, unlike a natural race, can receive a Crown. They

run their own race. The Crown that believers receive is very different than those of the world. The Heavenly Crowns rewarded, are Crowns that do not decay, nor rust, no moth, and it cannot be stolen. That's why JESUS said in Matt. 6:19, to store up treasures in heaven.

THE FIVE CROWNS

The Crown of Righteousness is given to those that love JESUS appearing when HE returns in the Rapture. (2 Timothy 4:8)

The Crown of Glory is given to the Faithful Under Shepherds, (Senior Pastors) that Shepherd the flock, under the CHIEF SHEPHERD, CHRIST JESUS. (1 Peter 5:4)

The Crown of Rejoicing is given to Soul Winners. (1 Thessalonians 2:19, Philippians 4:4) He that wins souls is wise. (Prov. 11:30)

The Crown of Life, is given to those that endure temptation, being faithful even unto death if necessary. (James 1:12, Rev. 2:10)

Imperishable Crown, given to those that are temperate, self-disciplined, self- controlled, keeping the body under subjection to CHRIST. (1 Corinthians 9:25-26, 1 Peter 1:4)

Review: The Great White Throne Judgment Unregenerate, Unjust Sinners, will stand before GOD and not JESUS. Why? Because they did not choose to accept the LORD JESUS CHRIST, as the WAY, the TRUTH, and the LIFE. Now, they must pay the wages of their own sins. They refused the Gift of GOD, which is Eternal Life through JESUS CHRIST the LORD. They will be judged for the sins they committed. Those that knew to do right but, didn't will be whipped with many stripes. In other words, they will suffer the greater damnation and punishment. Sinners are the only ones at the Great White Throne Judgment. They are there only to hear and learn the verdict: which is how hot the flames.

Hell was not created for mankind but for the devil and his demons. But, as the scriptures say, to whom you yield your body members to obey, that is your master. The people that will be at the Great White Throne Judgment decided. They yielded their members to Satan. They made a choice to obey his rebellious, self-righteous spirit. Therefore, he is their master and their master's punishment, they will share for all of eternity.

There is no party in hell. Friends will not be hooking up. It is a place of torment where the worm dies not. There is weeping and gnashing of teeth. There is torture, as sinners cry out in great anguish remembering and rehearsing over and over in their mind all of the opportunities that they passed up. The opportunities to accept, So Great a Salvation; rejected. Remember, JESUS said I stand at the door and knock. If any man hears my voice and open the door, I will come in and dine with HIM, and he with me." Isn't that what happened with Zacchaeus when he opened the door of HIS heart and house to JESUS? He ate with HIM. Zacchaeus came from that meal, a repented, saved and changed man.

Contrast to Zacchaeus, is the Rich Fool that didn't share with Lazarus but instead, built bigger barns. He, in some ways was like the Young Rich man that couldn't sell all he had and give it to the poor. They both trusted in something else to be their god. Those that will end up at the Great White Throne Judgment, have placed their trust in someone or something other than CHRIST JESUS the LORD. Their trust may be in people, or themselves. Maybe they believe that they are good enough apart from CHRIST. They could believe they can go to heaven because, they are a good person, etc. This is what we know, to be "dead works that equals filthy rags." Some may get caught up in the original sin that started in the Garden of Eden: believing a lie, from the father of lies, Satan himself. His trick was and still is the lust of the eyes, the lust of the flesh, and the pride of life. Now, in their rejecting of the SAVIOR, the ONE that loved them more than anyone, they are choosing to spend all of eternity separated from GOD. Hell will eventually be cast into the lake of fire. Therefore, the unbelievers will have their final abode in the lake of fire; living eternally is TORMENT! The teaching on how many Resurrections are there, Rewards, Crowns, where will the believers go for Judgment, where will the unbelievers go for their judgment, and what will they be judged on? Is so important. The Rooted & Grounded Bootcamp Book & Manual is a Must for everyone. I desire to have all Six Foundational Stones Laid Properly in everyone's life. That all will be Equipped, Rooted and Grounded on a Solid Foundation upon which to build their Faith. That all will become Bolder Disciples, ready, willing to Defend the Gospel, Properly Disciple others and be ready at JESUS' Return for them.

QUESTION & ANSWER WORKSHEET

1. After death then what? Fill in the blanks:
And as it is _____ unto men once to _____, then after this the _____. Scripture Reference: <u>Hebrews</u> 9:27.

2. Briefly Explain 1 Corinthians 15:51-53 and Revelations 11:15-19
_____
_____
_____
_____
_____
_____

3. Who is the Great White Throne of Judgment for? And who goes to the Judgment Seat of Christ?
_____
_____
_____
_____
_____
_____

4. What happens at the Judgment Seat of Christ?
_____
_____
_____
_____
_____
_____

5. What are the six works that Believers can produce?

_____
_____
_____
_____
_____

6. Which works will remain and why?

_____
_____
_____
_____

7. What are the Rewards described as in the Bible?

_____
_____
_____
_____
_____
_____

8. List the Five Crowns and to whom and why they are given.

_____
_____
_____
_____
_____

ASSESSMENT & REVIEW

1. Give your assessment of the Rooted & Grounded Boot Camp Book/Manual, the R&G One Day Conference, and Dr. Loretta Rich the Rooted and Grounded Bootcamp Founder and Teacher.

_____
_____
_____
_____
_____
_____

2. Do you believe that you were already properly Discipled in the Six Foundation Stones, please explain your answer.

_____
_____
_____
_____
_____
_____
_____

3. Would you recommend the Bootcamp Conference & the Book/Manual to others?

_____
_____
_____

4. With the R&G Boot Camp Manual as your guide, how GODfident (confident in GOD) are you in discipling others now,

_____
_____
_____
_____
_____
_____
_____
_____
_____

How To Order Rooted & Grounded Christian Believer's Bootcamp Book/ Manual

~Discount on Bulk Orders of Three or more
~Special on Books Ordered within the First 90 Days of Publishing

~Order Book(s) On

Amazon, Christian Books.com, Barnes & Nobles, or Order by Phone: (202) 880-0507 or (240) 435-9293

~Order through Cash App: $LRGBC5 or $KCMmin22
or
~Write: Loretta Rich Ministries
R&G Boot Camp
P.O. Box 783, Clinton
Maryland 20735
(Please Send Money Order, No Checks)

~Order Additional Copies for Your
~Church Leaders, New Members Orientation, Cell Small Groups, Family Discipleship or Family, Friends, Neighbors, and Personal Boot Camp Session, etc.

For More Information:
Email: loretta.rich@outlook.com
Text or Telephone: (202) 880-0507 or (240) 435-9293
Website: www.weightaside.org

THE RACE TO FINISH WELL HAS BEGUN!!! HAVE YOU THE CONFIDENCE TO PROPERLY DISCIPLE OTHERS? (MATTHEW 28:19)

Loretta Rich / ROOTED & GROUNDED
ONE DAY / BOOT-CAMP
CONFERENCE IS COMING YOUR WAY!!!
CONTACT FOR DETAILS IN YOUR AREA
ALL Are Welcome!
Register Now!!! For Discounts:
Early Registration, Group Size 3 + Registrations, Church, Cell Groups, & Church Leaders
(Registration Fee Covers: Registration, Conference, The R&G New Bootcamp Book/Manuel, Lunch, and Promotion Certificate)

LET'S GET READY AND DO THIS!!!
(John 9:4, Matthew 25:1-4)
We Do Not Know How Much Time We Have to Work Before CHRIST RETURNS for Us.
But We Do Know That HE Left Us a Command to Obey…
"GO MAKE DISCIPLES (Matthew 28:19)!" NOT JUST NEW CONVERTS.

REGISTRATION FORM

ROOTED & GROUNDED
ONE DAY / BOOT-CAMP
CONFERENCE

Your Promotion
IS JUST AROUND THE CORNER

For more information, Please Call / Text: (202) 880-0507 or (240) 435-9293 or Email: loretta.rich@outlook.com

Name: (First/M/Last):
_____

Age (circle one): 18-20 | 21 - 30 | 31 - 40 | 50 - 51+
Marital Status (circle one):
Single | Married | Divored | Widowed | Separated
Address (No P.O.B):
_____
_____

Phone Number (s): _____
Email _____
Church Affiliation (circle one): Yes | No If Yes, Name of Church:
_____
Senior Pastor: _____
Church Address: _____
    How long A Member: _____
        Spiritual Experience:
_____
_____

Church Work Experience:(Explain)
_____
_____

Goal(s) for Attending the Rooted & Grounded Bootcamp?
_____

Signature: _____
    Date: _____

www.ingramcontent.com/pod-product-compliance
Lightning Source LLC
Chambersburg PA
CBHW070508100426
42743CB00010B/1790